Sew It Yourself

Hardie Grant

BOOKS

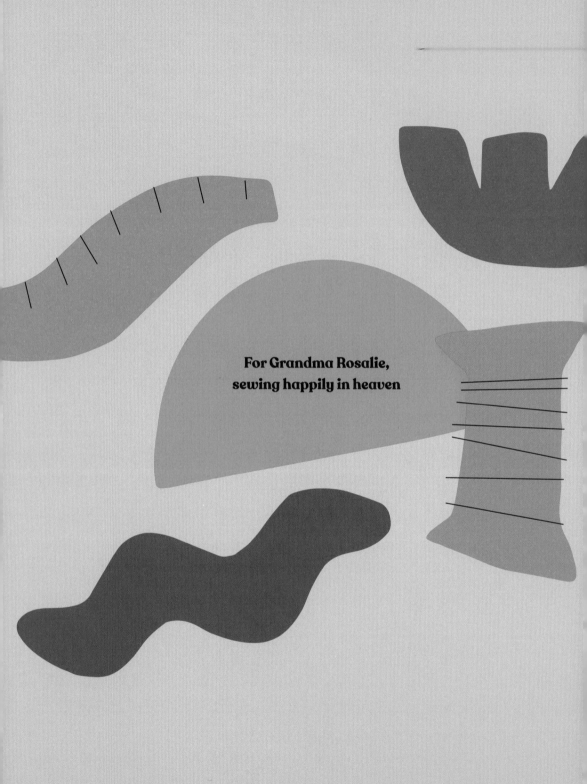

For Grandma Rosalie,
sewing happily in heaven

Daisy Braid

Sew It Yourself

20 pattern-free projects
(and infinite variations)
to make your dream wardrobe

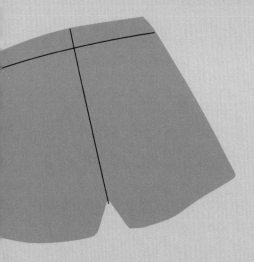

Contents

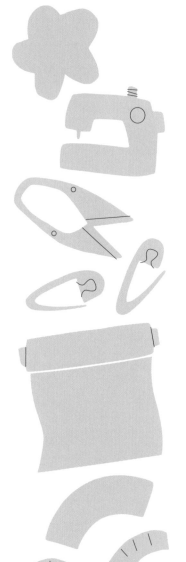

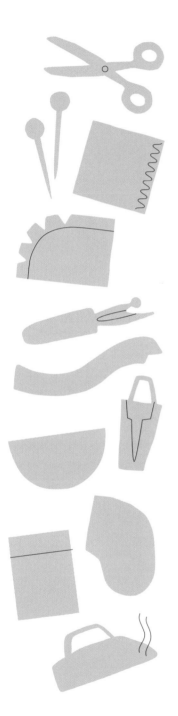

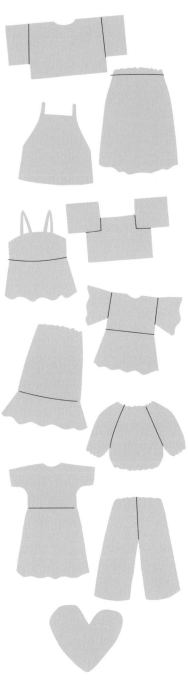

Part 3: Clothing Projects 129

Introduction

Hey maker, welcome! You might be reading this at the start of your sewing journey, or maybe you've been stitching away for years. Either way, I'm glad you're here.

This book is all about 'do it yourself' sewing — sewing for YOU. That means two things: sewing in a way that is fun and enjoyable for you (whether you're a beginner or more advanced sewist), and sewing clothes and accessories that make you feel like yourself when you wear them. You make the rules, choose the fabric, and decide just how big the sleeves will be (never big enough, in my opinion).

If you are new to sewing, my aim is to encourage you to give things a good old go. As a self-taught sewist, I folded, bunched, cut, and just put my foot down and stitched (almost destroying my grandmother's sewing machine along the way). When I didn't know something, I watched videos, read books and blogs, and chatted with sewing friends. If you aren't new to sewing, I hope this book serves as inspiration, not only for new sewing projects, but for new colour combinations, styling and fabric or simply a different approach to making clothes. When I lose my sewjo or get in a creative rut, trying something new or flicking through the pages of a crafty book can get my mind whirling again.

So what makes this book all about sewing it yourself, or rather sewing FOR yourself? For one thing, each of the twenty projects includes a variation that shows you how it can be altered, adjusted and hacked to make it your own.

The projects are also super easy to make because they're based on simple shapes and are constructed with no buttons, zips or darts. I think it's much easier to understand garment construction when you're starting out if you break things down into basic shapes. And then, when you see clothing in stores and on runways, you will start to think to yourself, *I can make that*, or even better, *I can make my own version of that*. And you can!

The garments and accessories featured in this book are easy to wear too – they are all loose-fitting, and you can just pull them over your head or slip them over your hips. Finally, there is only one size in this book: size YOU. The projects are each self-drafted, based on your own measurements; there are no patterns to trace, so you can customise each project to fit your body the way you want it to.

No matter where you are in your sewing journey, I hope this book inspires you to create something new, something unique, and something that is just for you. Make mistakes, try new styles and enjoy the process, then wear your handmade creations proudly. Practise saying, 'Thanks, I made it.'

This book is dedicated to all the people who inspired me to start sewing, motivated me to keep learning and supported my DIY journey. You might just find you're the reason someone else is inspired to start sewing too.

Daisy

Why I sew

Everyone has a different reason for sewing their own clothes and accessories. Here are a few of mine.

Fit and practicality

Ready-to-wear clothes aren't always a good fit – jeans can gape at the back and dresses can be too short. Tote bags can be too small, and too many things don't have pockets. I love to eat, move and create, so I like to wear comfortable clothing with no restrictions and to make accessories that are useful to me.

Creativity and self-care

I think everyone should have something that they do just for themselves. For me, sewing is a form of self-care and my creative outlet. I love how I feel when I transform flat pieces of fabric into something wearable – drawing lines, cutting, pinning and stitching pieces of fabric together to create something for yourself is extraordinary. I think all sewists will agree that when you try on your new creation it gives you a certain feeling: a combination of reward, satisfaction and excitement.

Personal style

Nothing is more unique than something you have made yourself. Sewing your own clothes allows you to be your own fashion designer and personal stylist. As your skills start to grow, your style might also develop. Making your own clothes means you can create exactly what you want to wear. When I started sewing my own clothes, I loved that what I made didn't exist anywhere else, and since then I have never felt more like myself.

Fashion revolution

The fashion industry is one of the world's biggest polluters. By creating my own clothes and accessories, I am in control of the waste I produce and the conditions in which things are made. Learning about the fashion industry gives you a greater appreciation for what goes into making garments. And until the global fashion industry puts an end to human and environmental exploitation, I will continue to make my own clothes and encourage others to learn how to do so. I think we all have a responsibility when creating a garment to do so in a sustainable and thoughtful way.

Community

I have made some great friends through the sewing community, both online and in person. Whenever I have a question, there is always someone keen to share their thoughts and skills. We celebrate not only our sewing wins but also our failures, learning from each other. I couldn't have written this book without the support of my sewing community!

TIP Whether your goal is to have an entirely me-made wardrobe or to create a one-off garment, it is essential to have an intention for your sewing. If you are pumping out a new outfit every day or for every event, is that any better than fast fashion? Consider how you might wear a garment in winter as well as in summer, or how it works with other pieces in your wardrobe. Can it be layered, and is it versatile? Think about what you might do with the scraps that a project produces: are they big enough to reuse as in-seam pockets or could they be stitched together to make a patchwork tote bag? Make things that you will wear over and over again. Outfit repeating is cool!

PART 1

Getting Started

How to Use This Book

Inside this book, you will find twenty DIY sewing projects (plus infinite variations) aimed at beginners but that can be made by sewists of all levels.

Before you start, it's important to familiarise yourself with the sewing techniques, terminology, tools and materials you will need to complete each project. In part 1 of the book (where we are now), you will find information about fabric, how to finish seams and measure your body, and lots more. Flip back here as much as you need to for technique tutorials and terminology.

After that, it's time to get sewing! In part 2, you will find accessory projects. These are a great starting point – they will allow you to practise and get the hang of techniques in straightforward, not-so-scary ways, before you apply them to bigger projects. They also use minimal fabric and some can be made with scraps or remnants. Part 3 is where you will find the clothing projects.

Think of the projects as a base or foundation: each of them can be altered, hacked and transformed however you'd like. Although each project comes with its own suggested variation, you can combine techniques from one project with another to create a whole new design. I encourage you to try on your me-mades throughout the sewing process – adjust the size of armholes or the length of skirts as you go to make sure each aspect works for you. Clothing can be constructed in many ways, and as you gain experience sewing different kinds of garments, you will learn new ways to create things.

Plan

Pick a project, read the instructions and choose any variations you might want to make.

Measure

Take your measurements and insert them into any formulas.

Fabric and thread

Pick a fabric that makes you smile and wind a bobbin with matching thread.

Mark and cut

Mark your shapes onto the fabric and cut them out.

Sew, snip and press

Sew everything together, snip loose threads and press the seams.

Wear and love

Try on your fabulous new handmade creation and wear it proudly.

Sewing safety and ergonomics

Sewing has many repetitive actions, and projects can take hours or days to complete. For your health and safety be mindful of the following when you sew:

- When cutting out fabric on the floor or a table or when you are sitting at the sewing machine, try to maintain a good posture.

- Always remember to turn off the iron after sewing! Mine automatically turns off after it's been left on for a while.

- When machine sewing, keep your fingers together and at least 3 cm (1 ¼ in) away from the presser foot and needle.

- Avoid sewing when you're tired, because sewing tools are sharp. Plus, even if you desperately want to finish a project, the results will be better when you're feeling refreshed.

TIP

Project make times are not listed in this book because the time it takes you to make a project will depend on your skill level and how much time you want to spend on a project. Try not to rush a sewing project. Well-made clothing will last a lot longer, and the more time and care put into making a garment, the better it will be!

Sewing Supplies and Fabrics

My teenage sewing experience was like being on *Project Runway* – trying to meet a design challenge of using a t-shirt, some fabric remnants and elastic to make a ball gown. I never did make a ball gown, but my teenage wardrobe *was* full of upcycled op shop finds and DIY creations that I made using fabric remnants from my aunt. I always found a way to put things together, even if some of my creations were a bit questionable. The challenge of making with what I had on hand was really fun, and I think learning how to sew in that way has made me the crafty maker I am today.

There are so many places to find fabric and other sewing supplies. Here are some of my suggestions.

Use what you have

You don't necessarily have to go out and buy supplies – often the best materials are the ones you already have. Old sheets and duvet covers are great for making toiles and practising other aspects of sewing. You can even dye them to give them a refresh. Maybe you have a pile of clothes that are damaged; could you use the fabric in them to make something new? As soon as my friends and family found out I like to sew, they started to offer me their old fabric stashes or extra supplies. I love seeing what they have stored away and being able to give it a new home and life by transforming it into something else.

When I visit fabric stores and see a fabric I like but don't yet have a project in mind, I usually buy 2–3 m (2 ¼–3 ¼ yd).

Second-hand

My favourite thing about buying second-hand fabric and sewing supplies is the hunt! Op shops, thrift stores and garage sales are treasure troves of affordable second-hand fabric and sewing supplies. Don't just look for bolts of fabric – you can also sew with bed sheets, tablecloths and curtains. You might have a one-of-a-kind creation made from the rare fabric of a bed sheet that hasn't been manufactured for thirty years!

Fabric stores

I enjoy shopping at fabric stores because you can touch and feel everything and compare products in person. Staff are often very knowledgeable about fabric and garment construction, so they can help you find something suitable for any project.

Online

If you don't live near a fabric store, you can shop online. Most companies offer a sampling service so you can check the fabric's colour, weight and feel before buying enough for a project.

Tools and supplies

When it comes to tools and basic supplies, there are a number of items that are essential to have in your sewing kit.

Sewing machine

As long as your machine can sew a straight stitch and a zigzag stitch, you can make all of the projects in this book. You don't need to go out and buy a fancy new machine. I got my machine second-hand and it's the best! Get familiar with your machine by reading the manual, watching videos online and reading reviews and blog posts. Before starting a project, test out your tension and stitch length on some scrap fabric.

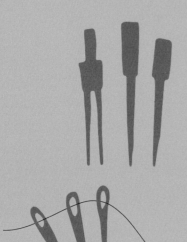

Sewing machine needles

There are lots of different types of sewing machine needles available. Universal needles will do the trick for most projects; however, it's best to check which size suits your sewing machine model and fabric. Some needles work better with knit fabrics, and some are super sharp, making them perfect for sewing delicate fabrics like silk.

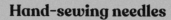

Hand-sewing needles

There isn't much hand sewing in this book, but you never know when one might come in handy!

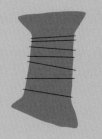

Thread

Cotton and polyester all-purpose threads are commonly used for sewing clothing and accessories. Choose the closest colour to your fabric, or slightly darker than your fabric if an exact match is not available.

Bobbins

A bobbin is a tiny spool that goes inside the bottom of your sewing machine and holds the thread that catches the top thread from the main spool, creating stitches. Check your machine manual to make sure you get the correct size. I like to have a couple of spares, so I don't have to unwind my full bobbins to sew with a new colour. Match the thread in the bobbin with the thread in the main spool for a clean finish.

Dressmaking pins

Pins are used to hold pieces of fabric together temporarily; they are like a pointy pair of extra hands. They come in different thicknesses, lengths and levels of sharpness, with plain or coloured ends and even cute shapes like flowers and stars. I prefer to use glass-headed pins because the plastic heads melt if I accidentally iron them! It's important to avoid sewing over pins as they can break your needle and damage your machine.

Pincushion or magnetic dish

Keep all of the pointy pin ends together by poking them into a pincushion or sticking them on a magnetic pin dish.

Measuring tape

A measuring tape is used to measure the body and curved edges. It's also a fantastic accessory to add to your outfit, so people know you sew.

Ruler

Super handy for measuring things and drawing lines and marks on your fabric, a ruler is a great tool to have when self-drafting. Don't have a ruler? Use the edge of a book instead to mark a straight line.

Washable marking tools

Mark out your self-drafted shapes with dressmaker's chalk or a fabric pencil or pen that's designed to wash out.

Sewing scissors

Invest in a good-quality pair of shears that can be sharpened; they will last you a lifetime. Remember, sewing scissors are only for cutting fabric!

Snips

Excellent for quickly snipping threads.

Elastic

Elastic is available in many different types and widths. For waistbands, I like to use non-roll elastic measuring from 2 ½ to 4 cm (1 to 1 ½ in) wide. For scrunchies and finishing puffy sleeves, I like knit elastic that measures 1 to 2 cm (½ to ¾ in) wide.

Safety pins

Use a safety pin to thread elastic through a casing.

Bias binding

Bias binding is a narrow strip of fabric used to finish raw edges such as necklines, armholes and seams, and it can also be used to make straps. See how to make continuous bias binding on page 56.

Bias binding tape maker

Speed up the process of making binding! Binding makers are available in a range of sizes; to make binding for the projects in this book, I suggest using an 18 mm or 25 mm (¾ in or 1 in) tape maker. If you're new to sewing, I recommend starting with a larger size.

Unpicker

An unpicker or seam ripper is used for unpicking seams. No matter how experienced you are at sewing, you will always need one of these.

Rotary cutter and cutting mat

A rotary cutter is very useful for tasks like cutting out strips of bias binding – but it should only be used on a cutting mat.

Overlocker

An overlocker or serger is often used to finish raw edges. It's not necessary, though it is an excellent investment and gives your projects a professional appearance.

Iron and ironing board

Iron out wrinkles after washing fabric by pressing down and moving the iron back and forth, as you would when ironing clothes. To help seams lie flat, gently press the iron onto seams in between steps; instead of moving the iron back and forth, lift the iron to move it onto the next section of the seam. Pressing seams will make your finished garment look more professional overall. Remember to change the heat setting depending on the fabric.

There are some extra things you might need that you probably already have: a pen or pencil, eraser, paper scissors and card stock for making templates.

Fabric

Picking a fabric is one of my favourite parts of making my clothes. Plain or printed, striped or checked – there are so many options to choose from. Fabric is an incredibly versatile material, and knowing how it's made will change the way you see clothes.

I like to sew with woven fabrics made from natural fibres. They are easy to handle and are lovely to wear all year round. Woven means that the fabric is non-stretchy, and when you are just starting out, I think it's the easiest to sew with.

There is so much more than meets the eye when it comes to fabric! Here's a few basics to know.

Weave and grain

Woven fabric is made by weaving two threads together: a warp and a weft. The selvedge is the ribbon-like edge on either side of the fabric. The weft threads run from left to right and are known as the crosswise grain. The warp threads create the lengthwise grain and run parallel to the selvedge. The lengthwise grain is often known as the grainline.

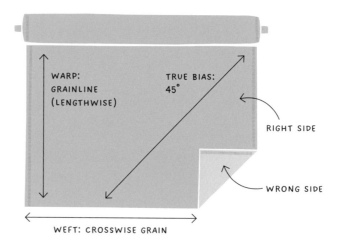

WARP:
GRAINLINE
(LENGTHWISE)

TRUE BIAS:
45°

RIGHT SIDE

WRONG SIDE

WEFT: CROSSWISE GRAIN

The garments in this book are all cut on the grainline, and this direction will be indicated with an arrow on every illustrated pattern piece, which is the same symbol you will see on paper patterns. It's important to cut all of your pattern pieces in the same direction, especially with directional prints. If you cut them on different grains, they will drape differently.

The bias grain or true bias is the line that runs through the fabric at a 45-degree angle to the selvedge. When fabric is cut on this angle, it has maximum give and stretch and is perfect for making bias binding and bias-cut garments.

Directional fabric

Some fabrics have a print or texture that goes in one direction, known as the nap – for example, a fabric where all the flowers are pointing upwards. When cutting fabrics like this, be sure to cut your pattern pieces so that the print runs in the same direction. Otherwise, your garment will have prints facing both up and down. (When I do this, I like to call it an unintentional intentional design choice.)

Right and wrong side

The front of the fabric is referred to as the right side – this is the side that shows on the outside of a garment. The back of the fabric is referred to as the wrong side and will be illustrated in this book with a lighter shade of colour. When you're working with a printed fabric, it's easy to identify the right and wrong sides, whereas it isn't so obvious on plain fabrics. If you are unsure, pick a side that you want to be the right side and mark that side with chalk when you cut out your pattern pieces.

Types of fabric

Any lightweight or midweight woven fabric will work for these projects, and many could be adapted and made in knit (stretchy) fabrics. The choice is yours! Here are my top woven fabric picks for my DIY creations. Unless stated, these are recommended fabrics to use for all of the projects throughout the book.

Cotton lawn

My favourite fabric for all of my DIY designs is cotton lawn. It's a lightweight fabric with a crisp finish and a beautiful buttery, smooth sheen due to its tight weave.

Cotton poplin

Slightly heavier than a lawn, cotton poplin is a strong, crisp fabric that suits many projects. It comes in lots of colours and is super easy to cut and sew.

Cotton voile

Voiles can be 100% cotton or a blend; they are super lightweight and a little bit sheer. When sewing with this fabric, make sure you have sharp pins and a fresh needle, and test the tension of your stitches on a scrap of the fabric before you start sewing to make sure it's just right.

Cotton canvas

Canvas is durable, sturdy and available in a range of weights. A lightweight canvas is great for garment sewing – think voluminous Trace Pants (see page 199) and the big crispy ruffles on the Wrap Bib (see page 172).

Linen

Easy to care for and beautiful to wear, I love how lightweight to midweight linen relaxes and softens after every wash. It's such a casual yet luxurious fabric and comes in so many colours.

Silk crepe de chine

If you want to sew with silk, crepe de chine is a great step up once you have the hang of sewing cotton. Tightly woven like cotton lawn, this silk has a matt finish, so it doesn't slip around too much. Take your time when cutting this fabric, as it is a little bit trickier to handle, and don't forget to use a sharp needle.

Wool

Lightweight woven fabrics made from wool can be used to make clothing with extra built-in warmth.

 TIP
You might like to make a toile (pronounced 'twahl') or muslin out of cheap or second-hand fabric when starting a new project to make sure the garment fits correctly. It enables you to take notes of your measurements and the adjustments you make so that the next time you sew up the project, it will fit better. Making a toile is also a great way to practise the techniques used in a project. You don't always have to sew the bias binding or facings as well, but do try to use fabric of similar weight to the fabric you plan to sew with. If you don't intend to wear a toile, using a longer stitch length will speed up the sewing process.

Storing and preparing fabric

If you have started to collect a stash of fabric, you will have to choose a way to store it.

It's good to get into the habit of pre-washing new fabric as soon as you get home so that it's ready to use when inspiration hits — then you can cut straight into it! Washing your fabric before sewing is essential to get rid of any shrinkage. Not all fabrics will shrink, and often it's only a tiny amount, but it's better to eliminate shrinkage before sewing rather than after because your garment may no longer fit you. Wash your fabric the same way you intend to wash it once it has been sewn up. When your fabric has dried, iron it using the appropriate level of heat to remove any creases or wrinkles.

Then you can store your fabric by:

- hanging it on clothes hangers
- folding and stacking it in a cupboard
- rolling and tying it with a strip of fabric or a rubber band.

Write a tag listing the length of the fabric and its composition, and pin or tie it to the fabric to refer to later. You might also want to consider keeping swatches of your fabric stash in a notebook to make keeping track of what you have even easier.

 TIP If you have an overlocker, finish the cut edges on your fabric before pre-washing to stop them from fraying.

Sewing Basics and Techniques

It's almost time to get sewing, but before you do, it's important you get an idea of the sewing techniques and terminology that will be used for the projects in this book. Each project will mention the techniques but won't explain the complete process, so you will need to refer to the instructions in this section.

Whenever you start a new craft, creative hobby or project, there will always be scary feelings and moments of doubt. Making mistakes or not making sense of instructions can be discouraging – it's like learning a new language. But don't give up! When I started sewing, my seams were wonky, and I used the unpicker more than I would have liked, but I still loved the things that I was making because I was making them for myself. Your sewing journey has to start somewhere, and your confidence will grow every time you learn a new technique or finish a project.

TIP

'Sewjo' is a term used in the sewing community to describe your sewing mojo. It's your motivation to sew or the inspiration to create and make. Sometimes you will lose your sewjo, and that's okay! Don't force it, just go with the flow. My sewjo comes back when I take a break; I might tidy a space, cook a meal, read a book or listen to a good podcast. If you are frustrated and lose your sewjo, put down your sewing and return to it when you're in the mood and have the energy.

Shapes and formulas

Sewing is all about shapes. Nearly every project starts with a rectangle (sew two together and you pretty much have a tote bag). Semicircles are cut away to reveal neck holes, and triangles are cut out to make armholes.

Instead of giving you patterns to trace, this book provides formulas to create the shapes (or pattern pieces) used to construct garments. At the start of each project is a list of the shapes needed to create that project, as well as the formulas to calculate the dimensions of those shapes. Just draw the shapes onto your fabric based on your body measurements or the measurements provided. Don't be scared off by the word 'formula'. Think of it like a recipe – there is no tricky maths here!

To work out the width of a shape, the formula takes a body measurement, divides it by two, and then adds ease and seam allowance, like this:

Width = body measurement ÷ 2 + ease + seam allowance

To work out the height of a shape, the formula takes a body measurement and adds a casing, hem or seam allowance, like this:

Height = body measurement + casing/hem/seam allowance

'Ease' is the amount of extra fabric you will add to your pattern pieces beyond your body's measurements. It ensures a garment will sit well and fit comfortably, and allows your body to move, grow and change throughout the day. The seam allowance is how much fabric you will leave to stitch your seams.

The measurements that are calculated from these two formulas are then used to create the pattern piece:

Width x height = shape/pattern piece

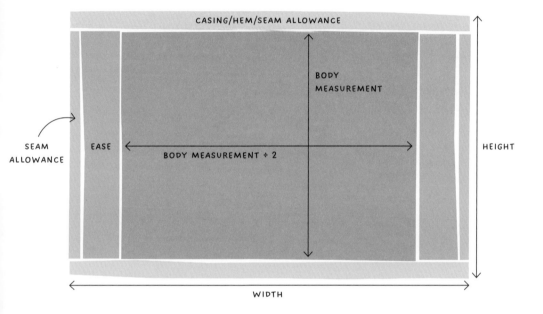

TIP

Plan what a project is going to look like by drawing a sketch. It's great to visualise your goal so you have something to refer back to as you work on a project. I'm not a great illustrator but I love to put my ideas onto paper first.

How to take your measurements

Take your measurements with a measuring tape, holding it horizontal or vertical as needed, and measure around your body while standing in a natural position. Keep the tape taut but not tight and let it follow the curves of your body.

1. Arm bust

Measure around your body including your arms at the fullest point of your bust with your arms down by your sides. Your bust at its fullest point is usually over your nipples.

2. High bust

Measure around your chest with the tape measure just under your armpits and above your bust.

3. Full bust

Measure around your chest at the fullest point of your bust.

4. Full waist

Measure around your waist at the narrowest point.

5. Full hips

Measure around your hips at the fullest point.

6. Waist to knee

Measure from your waist at the narrowest point down to just above or on your knee.

7. Top of shoulder to full bust

Measure from the top of your shoulder where it meets your neck down to the fullest part of your bust.

8. Top of shoulder to under bust

Measure from the top of your shoulder where it meets your neck down to under your bust.

9. Waist to hip

Measure from your waist at the narrowest point to your hips at the fullest point.

10. High bust to belly button or knees

Measure from your high bust down the front of your body to the desired length.

11. Top of shoulder to waist or hip

Measure from the top of your shoulder where it meets your neck down the front of your body to the desired length.

12. Edge of shoulder to elbow

Measure from the edge of your shoulder down your arm to your elbow.

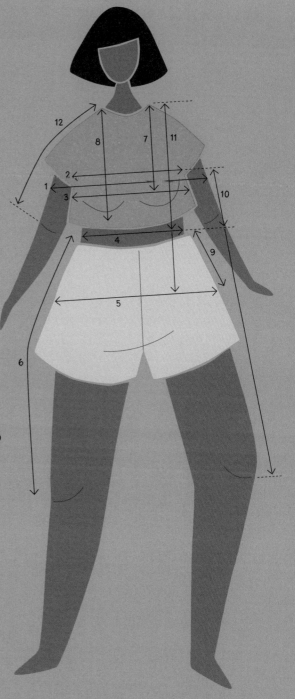

How to calculate how much fabric you need

Each project calls for different amounts of fabric, and the amount required will depend on your measurements and the width of the fabric. To determine how much fabric you need for the projects in this book – whether you already have the fabric and want to check you have enough, or need to know how much to buy – use a pattern-cutting layout. Your ruler will come in handy here!

When you buy a paper pattern, a pattern-cutting layout is provided that outlines the most economical or efficient way of cutting out the pattern pieces. I don't provide cutting layouts for each project here but encourage you to determine the best layout for you and your chosen fabric. It's simple to create your own based on the fabric you have in your stash or that you plan to buy. I'm a very visual creator, and I like to sketch and plan out my pattern-cutting layouts. The method given on the following pages works well with the projects in this book because they are made with simple shapes, with mostly straight edges.

Rectangle width = Width ÷ 10
Rectangle height = Length ÷ 10

A sheet of paper or card

1. To calculate how much fabric you will need, first take your measurements and insert them into the formulas provided for your chosen project. Now you know the dimensions of your pattern pieces.

2. If you already have fabric, use a pencil and paper to draw a rectangle that is a scaled-down version of the piece of fabric using the formula on page 40, dividing the measurements by 10. For example, if your fabric is 140 cm (55 ¼ in) wide and 2 m (2 ¼ yd) long, draw a rectangle 14 cm (5 ½ in) wide and 20 cm (8 in) high. If you need to determine how much fabric to buy, work on the basis of a standard fabric width like 110 cm (43 ¼ in) or 135 cm (53 ¼ in) and leave the rectangle open at one end.

3. Next, scale down the pattern pieces using the same formula, dividing by 10, and arrange them inside your 'fabric' rectangle in a way that you think fits efficiently. Remember to place them all aligned in the same direction.

4. Once you have drawn all the required pattern pieces, measure the length the combined pieces cover (or add up the heights) and use the formula in reverse, multiplying the number by 10: this will give you a rough fabric length. In the example opposite, the scaled-down heights add up to 15 cm (6 in), meaning you would need roughly 1 ½ m (1 ⅔ yd) of fabric.

TIP
There is a famous saying in the sewing world: 'Measure twice, cut once.' This saying can also apply to double-checking your formula results if they don't look right or that the pieces are all the right way around when you are cutting a directional fabric. But I always buy a little extra fabric in case my calculations are off or I make a mistake.

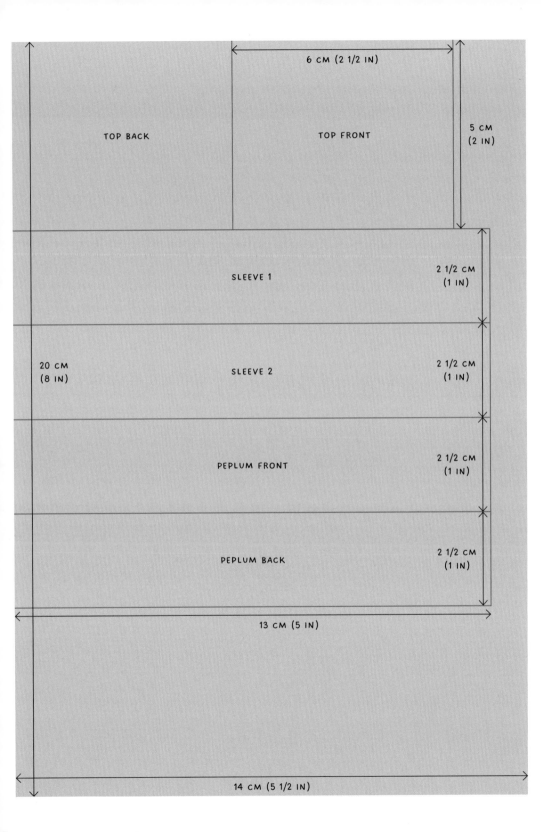

6 CM (2 1/2 IN)

TOP BACK

TOP FRONT

5 CM
(2 IN)

SLEEVE 1

2 1/2 CM
(1 IN)

20 CM
(8 IN)

SLEEVE 2

2 1/2 CM
(1 IN)

PEPLUM FRONT

2 1/2 CM
(1 IN)

PEPLUM BACK

2 1/2 CM
(1 IN)

13 CM (5 IN)

14 CM (5 1/2 IN)

How to cut out pattern pieces

When cutting out pattern pieces, lay out the fabric nice and flat on a large clear surface. Decide if you are going to mark out each piece individually or fold your fabric in half lengthways to cut out your pieces on the fold. The approach you take will depend on how much fabric you have and how you have planned the pattern layout (see page 40). It's helpful to plan a pattern layout before cutting pattern pieces so that you can find the most efficient use of fabric. I like to cut out my pieces when the fabric is folded in half because it means I only have to cut once. Use a washable marking tool and ruler to measure and mark out the shapes required for your project. Once you have marked out all of your pattern pieces, cut them out carefully.

How to pin pattern pieces

After you've cut out your pattern pieces, pinning helps to closely align seams, which will result in a better finish overall. There are a bunch of ways you can pin pattern pieces together. My pinning style is to insert them perpendicular to the edge of the fabric so I can take them out easily when sewing. Another way is to pin parallel with the edge of the fabric, though you need to make sure the points of the pins are facing away from you when you're sewing so you can remove the pins before the presser foot runs over them! A good rule of thumb is to place a pin every 5 cm (2 in) when sewing straight seams but closer when it's a more fiddly fabric or part of a process like binding a neckline.

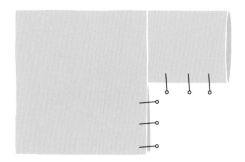

How to sew a seam

Seams hold all sewing projects together and are sewn at the edge of the seam allowance, which is the space between the edge of the fabric and the line of stitches. The seam allowance used for all projects in this book is 1 cm (½ in) unless stated otherwise.

There are many ways to sew a seam; the stitches used for the types of seams that appear in this book are listed below.

Straight stitch

The most common stitch used to sew woven fabric is the straight stitch. A 2 ½ mm (⅛ in) stitch length is the standard for sewing most garments. When sewing a straight seam, use the edge of the foot as a guide: line it up with the edge of the fabric to help you sew a consistently straight line.

Backstitch

Backstitching is when you straight stitch in reverse for about 3–5 stitches, and it's used to secure the beginning and end of a row of stitching. Most machines have a button or lever that you can press while sewing to make the machine reverse. Get into the habit of backstitching at the start and end of your seams.

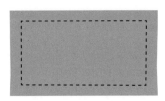

Topstitch

Topstitching is straight stitching that is visible on the outside of a garment. It's usually used to hold facing in place or as a decorative stitch.

Edgestitch

Edgestitching keeps finished edges lying flat; it is a straight stitch sewn very close to the edge.

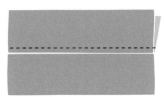

Understitch

Understitching is a straight stitch made to the seam allowance on the facing of a garment to stop the facing from rolling out.

Staystitch

This is a straight stitch sewn on a curved edge to prevent the curve from stretching. It's often used on necklines and hems cut in a curve or on the bias.

Basting stitch

A basting stitch is a long stitch used to hold two or more layers of fabric together temporarily.

How to finish a seam

There are several ways to finish a seam to prevent the fabric from fraying and help your creations last longer. Cotton lawns and poplins are so tightly woven that they don't often fray in the wash, but linen definitely needs something to keep it under control. Some projects may even involve a combination of different seam finishes. Whichever method you choose to finish a seam, and whether you choose to finish a seam at all, is totally up to you. The tutorials in this book won't tell you how to finish your seams every time, so choose the method you like the most to finish your seams.

Pinking shears

The simplest way to finish a seam is to use pinking shears and cut along the edge of the seam allowance. This method is fast and easy; however, it isn't the most effective, and loosely woven fabrics like linen may still fray in the wash.

Zigzag

A zigzag stitch is a simple go-to finish to prevent seams from fraying if you don't have an overlocker. Set the width of the stitches at medium to wide and sew along the edge of your seam allowance while avoiding sewing over the stitch line.

French seams

French seams are a kind of self-enclosed seam and are often used on garments that will get a lot of wear or when sewing more delicate fabric. The basic process of sewing a French seam is described below; if you want to reduce waste, reduce the seam allowance so that trimming is not required.

1. With the wrong sides of the fabric together, stitch the seam 5 mm (¼ in) from the edge. Trim 2 mm (⅛ in) from the seam allowance, being careful not to cut into the stitching.

2. Open up the fabric and press the seam to one side. Fold the fabric with the right sides together, making sure the seam is along the fold. Press again.

3. Stitch 5 mm (¼ in) from the edge of the fabric, open it up and press. The raw edges will be enclosed inside the seam, and they will be nice and strong.

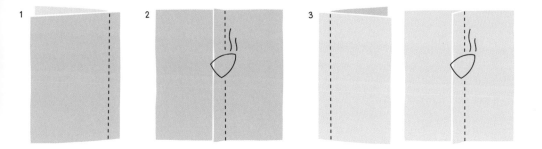

Bias-bound seams

Bias binding is a narrow strip of fabric cut on the bias grain that is used to finish raw edges. Fabric cut on the bias stretches, so it is great for curving around seams like necklines and armholes (also known as armscyes). Bias binding can also bind the raw edges on seams when sewing a French seam is tricky. Simply sandwich the raw edge inside double fold binding and stitch along the edge of the binding to secure it. I will talk more about bias binding on page 56.

Overlocker or serger

An overlocker is a machine that trims the edge of the fabric while creating stitches by looping threads along the edge of the fabric to encase the raw edge. You will have seen this finish inside ready-to-wear clothing. Overlockers are a great investment, but are not necessary to make great garments.

How to clip and notch curved seams

Reduce bulk and help curved seams lie better by clipping or notching the seam allowance.

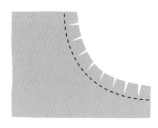

Clipping seams

Use this method for concave curves on underarms and necklines. To clip a seam, make a straight snip into the seam allowance, stopping before the line of stitches.

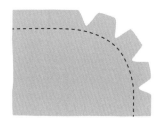

Notching seams

Notch a seam if it is a convex curve. Cut a small triangle of fabric out of the seam allowance, stopping before the line of stitches.

TIP

What's the difference between ironing and pressing? Ironing is when you move the iron back and forth on top of the fabric to smooth out creases and wrinkles. Ironing fabric before cutting out pattern pieces will make matching up seams easier. Pressing, however, is achieved with an up and down motion: you gently press the iron down on a seam before lifting it straight up off the fabric, and continue along a seam in this way. It's important not to 'iron' fabrics during the sewing process as you risk distorting the grain of the fabric, which can make a difference in the shape or size of your finished garment. Pressing eliminates the risk of distorting the fabric before it has been sewn up and finished.

How to gather

Gathering draws a piece of fabric into puckers so it will fit into a smaller area, and it's the technique used to create ruffles on all of the projects in this book. It involves adjusting the stitch length to the longest length and tension to the loosest option to sew a basting stitch. Backstitching is not required when you sew gathering stitches because you will need to spread and move the fabric along the threads. A gathering foot is available for most machines but is not essential for achieving fabulous ruffly results.

1. Turn your machine to its longest stitch length and loosest stitch tension. Test this on a scrap piece of fabric; I like to sew gathering on the longest and loosest option, but you can adjust this depending on your machine and the fabric you are using. Pull out a long tail of thread – about 10–15 cm (4–6 in) long – from both the top spool and bobbin threads.

2. On the right side of the fabric, sew a straight line 5 mm (¼ in) from the edge of the fabric. Your machine may start to gather the fabric by itself, so after sewing this first line, spread out the fabric again. Then sew a second straight line 1 cm (½ in) from the edge of the fabric. When you reach the end, leave a long tail of thread in case you need to spread the gathers more.

3. Gently pull either both of the spool or both of the bobbin strings to tighten the gathers, or spread the puckering along the stitches until the gathered fabric reaches the length required. Then pin it onto your garment or accessory with the right sides together and stitch along the edge to attach it. Once you have attached your gathered fabric, you may still be able to see the gathering stitches, but don't worry – these can be unpicked when the garment is complete.

TIP

Before you begin sewing a gather, check you have enough thread on the spool and bobbin. Gathering uses up a lot of thread, and it's annoying to run out halfway through a seam.

2

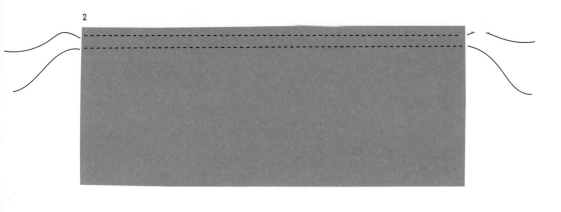

3

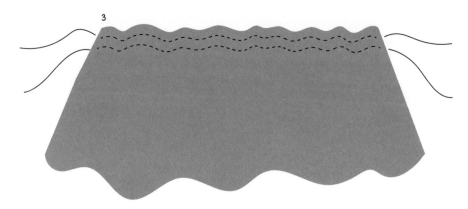

How to unpick a seam

If you are reading this page, you might have made a mistake that requires unpicking. You may have sewn the bias binding to the sleeve hole when planning to attach sleeves, or maybe you have sewn your pattern pieces upside down. It's okay! Don't worry – all sewists have been there, and it's just part of the learning process.

There are many ways to undo your mistakes. Always use a seam ripper slowly and carefully. Start by unpicking the backstitching and remember to rip away from your body. Depending on the kind of fabric, you may alter the method you use to unpick seams.

 TIP Worried you won't be able to sew in a straight line? Try sewing with a plaid or gingham fabric. The lines in the fabric will help you keep your seams straight.

Seam splitting

This method is my favourite as it's suitable for most fabrics. After unpicking the backstitching, gently pull the two pieces of fabric apart and insert the seam ripper below the ladder of stitches that have appeared. Push the blade through until you have cut the first few stitches, and then pull the fabric apart again. Repeat until you reach the end of the seam.

Every third, fourth or fifth stitch

My second favourite method is to unpick every third, fourth or fifth stitch on one side of the fabric. Then turn the fabric over and pull the thread, unpicking the seam. Great for delicate fabrics.

Plowing

Plowing is similar to seam splitting and can be used with sturdier heavyweight fabrics; if not done carefully, it can rip the fabric. With the red ball facing down, place the seam ripper between the two pieces of fabric. Hold the fabric taut and then push (or plow) the seam ripper through the seam until you get to the end.

How to make continuous bias binding

Bias binding is used in many projects throughout the book and is available ready-made in most sewing and fabric supply stores; however, it is relatively easy to make at home and is a great scrap buster. I suggest using double fold bias binding for the projects in this book, so here is how you make it in one continuous strip, both with and without a bias tape maker.

With a 25 mm (1 in) bias tape maker

1. To make double fold bias binding, you will first make single fold bias binding. To get started, double the number marked on the bias tape maker. If you are using a 25 mm tool, you will need to cut out strips 5 cm (2 in) wide. Using a ruler, mark lines on the bias grain 5 cm (2 in) wide and cut them out using scissors or a rotary cutter.

2. Cut the ends of the strips to a 90-degree angle. With right sides together, overlap the ends of two bias pieces at right angles and pin.

3. Draw a diagonal line through the imaginary square that the two overlapping strips have created and sew along this line, backstitching at the beginning and the end.

4. Trim along the seam allowance to reduce bulk, then press the seam allowance open.

5. Repeat steps 2–4 with the remaining strips until you have one long strip.

6. Cut one end of the long strip into a point and push it through the wide end of the bias tape maker with the wrong side facing up. Use a pin or something pokey to help you pull it through.

7. Once it's coming through the other side, manoeuvre the fabric so that the strip is centred and the edges are starting to curve over.

8. On your ironing board, slowly pull out the binding and iron the folds the tape maker has created.

9. Once you have finished pulling all of the binding through, fold it in half again and iron so that you have double fold binding with a finished width of 12.5 mm (½ in).

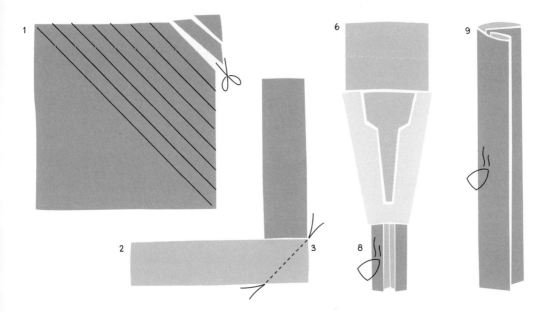

Without a bias tape maker

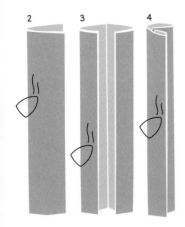

1. Follow steps 1–5 on the opposite page.

2. Fold the strip of fabric in half with the wrong sides facing and press.

3. Open it out, fold the outside edges into the centre line and press.

4. Finish by folding it in half and ironing it again.

Make bias binding with a fabric of the same weight or slightly lighter than what you are using to sew your project. Avoid making bias binding from heavyweight fabrics as it will be difficult to make and sew through.

How to apply bias binding

The sandwich method

With this method, the binding is visible on the outside of the garment. If I'm using this method, I match the binding to the fabric.

1. Sandwich the raw edge between the folds of the bias binding and pin.

2. Edgestitch along the edge of the bias binding. Press.

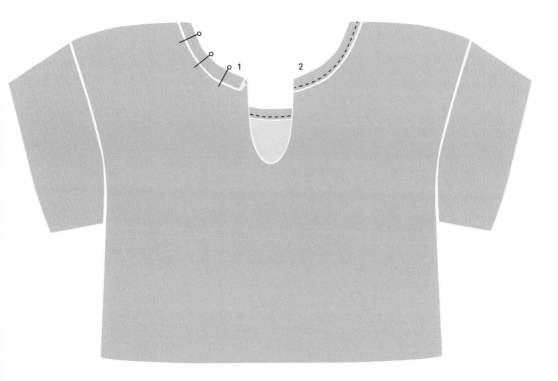

The facing method

With this method, the binding is not visible on the outside of the garment – only a line of stitching is seen. If I'm applying this method, I like to use a contrasting binding.

1. Open out the binding and align the raw edge with the raw edge you are finishing with right sides together and pin. Sew along the fold line and remove pins as you go. Be careful not to stretch the binding as you sew.

2. On the wrong side of the garment, press the seam allowance towards the bias tape.

3. Fold the binding over so the wrong sides are facing, lining up the edge of the binding with the line you just stitched. Press. Fold over the binding again, enclosing all raw edges, and edgestitch in place.

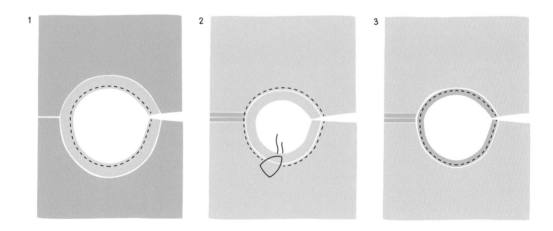

How to make a neckline template

One of the trickiest parts about self-drafting is getting the neckline just right. When I started self-drafting, I always cut my necklines too big, and my tops kept slipping off my shoulders! When I finally found a pattern with a neckline I liked, I traced it so I could use it again and again.

If you don't have a pattern you can trace, you can also make a template from a top or dress in your wardrobe that has a neckline you love. Alternatively, you can trace the template from the inside cover of this book, make a toile to test the fit and adjust as needed to suit you.

The instructions here create a template with a complete neck outline; if you are cutting fabric on the fold, remember to fold the template in half.

YOU WILL NEED

An A4 sheet of paper or card

A top or dress made from a woven fabric that has a round neckline you like

TIP

Punch a hole in your template and keep it hanging around on some twine.

1. Fold your paper in half and mark a line 1 cm (½ in) down from the top edge. This will be the seam allowance.

2. Take your top and fold it in half along the centre front. Place the top onto the paper, aligning the centre front fold with the fold on the paper. The shoulder seam of the top should line up with the 1 cm (½ in) line on the paper.

3. Trace along the front neckline. Take the top away and continue drawing the line up to the top edge of the paper. Now it includes a 1 cm (½ in) seam allowance.

4. Turn the paper upside down and mark a line 1 cm (½ in) down from the top edge for the seam allowance. Fold the top in half along the centre back and repeat steps 2 and 3 with the back necklines.

5. Cut out the two neck holes, unfold the paper and sticky tape the shapes together. This is the template that includes both the front and the back neckline. You can trace this template onto sturdier paper or card to make your template stronger.

6. Make a toile to test the fit and adjust the template as necessary.

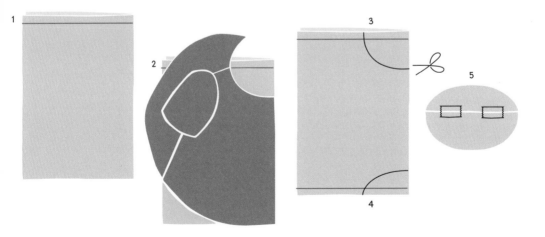

How to make a casing

A casing is a tunnel sewn into a garment to enclose a drawstring or elastic. In this book I use self-fabric casings, which means the casing is included in the design and measurements of the project. The height of a casing will depend on the width of your elastic, so I like to make a template using a piece of card.

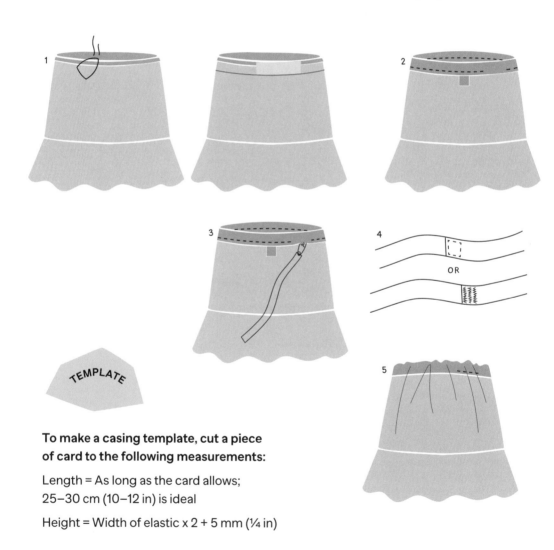

To make a casing template, cut a piece of card to the following measurements:

Length = As long as the card allows; 25–30 cm (10–12 in) is ideal

Height = Width of elastic x 2 + 5 mm (¼ in)

1. Fold the garment edge over 5 mm (¼ in) to the wrong side and press. On the wrong side of the fabric and using the template, trace or mark a line along the top pressed edge of the project all the way around.

2. Fold the top edge to the line and pin. If you are sewing a waistband, now is the time to add a label (see page 72): place it under the waistband at the centre back and pin it in place. Sew a straight stitch along the casing edge, leaving a gap about 5 cm (2 in) wide to insert elastic.

3. Pin one end of the elastic near the hole so it won't get pulled all the way through. Attach a large safety pin to the other end of the elastic and insert it through the hole. Guide it through the casing all the way around until it reaches the hole again.

4. Overlap the ends of the elastic by about 2 cm (¾ in) and pin together with the safety pin. Make sure the elastic isn't twisted inside the casing. Try on the garment and adjust the length of the elastic if required. Stitch the elastic ends together with a zigzag stitch, going back and forth a couple of times to make it nice and secure.

5. Push the elastic inside the casing, stitch up the hole and snip loose threads.

 You can also use the casing template as a template for hems.

How to make in-seam pockets

When I first started sewing I was afraid to tackle adding pockets, but after reading a couple of tutorials I found out that it is actually pretty easy. And it makes the finished creation way more practical! I don't add pockets to all my clothing projects – I tend to carry a tote wherever I go, which holds everything I need – but I always love a garment more when I do.

In-seam pockets are sewn into the side seam of a garment, so if you want to include them you need to plan them at the start of a project. You can cut them in the same fabric as your garment or use leftover fabric from another project, or even sew multiple smaller pieces together to make the size you need. They are a great scrap buster! In-seam pockets can be added to any of the projects in this book (the tutorial on the following pages is shown using the Sophie Trapezoid Skirt; see page 139) – just remember to sew them onto your pattern pieces before you sew up the side seams. These pockets are usually placed between the waist and the hip: use the formulas below as a guide for where to put them to suit your height and desired placement. (D) stands for the distance from the top edge of the garment to the top of the pocket.

Placement for projects with an elastic waistband:

(D) = Waist to hip + (width of elastic x 2 + 1 cm/½ in)

Placement for projects with a gathered skirt that drops from the waist:

(D) = Waist to hip + seam allowance

In-seam pocket template (see inside cover)

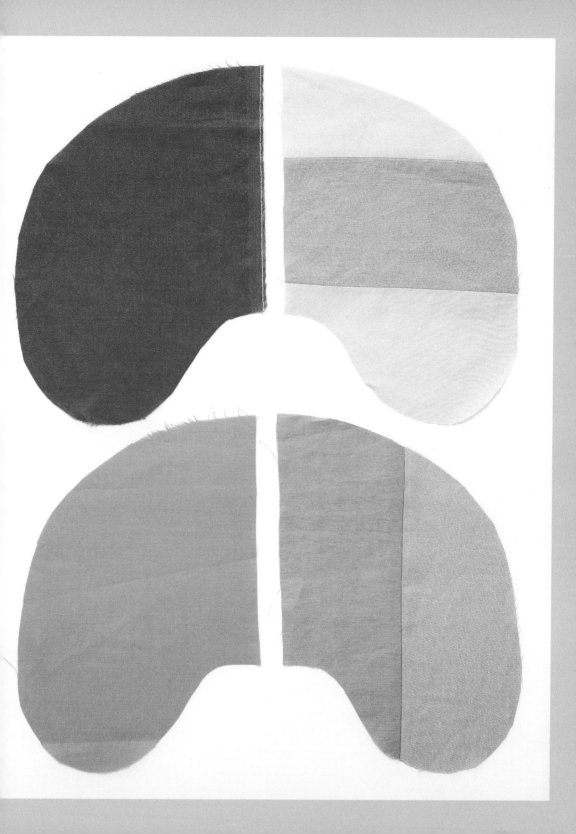

1. Trace the pocket template from the inside cover of this book onto a piece of paper. Place the template onto your fabric and cut four pattern pieces. Finish the edges of each pocket piece and the sides of the skirt or other garment, back and front, with a zigzag stitch or on an overlocker.

2. Mark where the pocket will start using the formulas on page 66. Place a pocket piece on each side of the garment front with right sides together, lining up the top edge of each pocket with the marks you just made, and pin. Sew along the edge of the pockets to attach them to the garment front with a 5 mm (¼ in) seam allowance. Repeat by marking and sewing the remaining two pocket pieces to the pattern piece for the back of the garment.

3. Fold the pockets out and press the seam allowance towards the pocket. Understitch the seam allowance to the pocket to stop it from rolling out when the project is finished.

4. Lay the garment front on the garment back with right sides together and pin the side seams, including the pockets. Sew down the side seams and around the pockets.

5. Turn out the garment, push the pockets inside and press. Then you can go ahead and finish the garment.

How to make patch pockets

Patch pockets are great for when you don't want to add bulk to the side seams of a project. You can add a patch pocket in almost any shape you'd like, but I've stuck to a classic rectangle pocket, made by tracing this book.

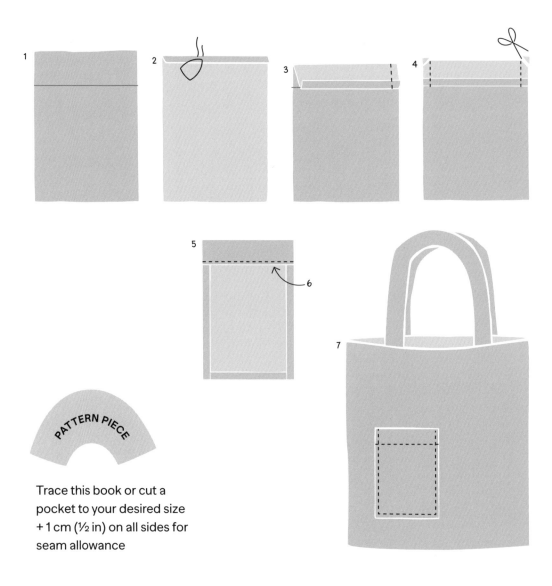

Trace this book or cut a pocket to your desired size + 1 cm (½ in) on all sides for seam allowance

1. Mark a line on the right side of the fabric 5 cm (2 in) from the top edge.

2. Turn the pocket over, so the right side is facing down. Fold the top edge of the pocket over by 1 cm (½ in) with wrong sides facing and press.

3. Turn the pocket over so the wrong side is facing down and fold the top edge to the line you marked in step 1 and pin it in place. Sew a straight stitch down both sides with a 1½ cm (½ in) seam allowance to fix the fold in place.

4. Trim diagonally across the corners at the top to reduce bulk.

5. Turn out the top fold so it is right side out – use the end of a pencil or your finger to poke out the corners. The sides of the pocket should turn under on their own, wrong sides together, along the stitch line. Iron the top fold and the sides flat along the stitch line. Fold up the bottom edge by 1½ cm (½ in) and iron flat.

6. Topstitch the top fold down.

7. Pin the pocket in position and sew around the side and bottom edges in one continuous seam. Pivot at the corners by lifting the presser foot while the needle is down and turning (pivoting) the fabric. Then lower the presser foot and continue the seam.

How to sew a label on a handmade creation

Adding a label to your handmade creation is like signing your name in the corner when you finish a painting. You can purchase woven labels from most fabric stores or design your own online. Alternatively, you can make your own using fabric scraps, bias binding or offcuts. And you can sew them anywhere! Sew them into the side seam for a little cheeky peek on the outside, into the waistband to indicate the back of a garment, or below the back neckline for that classic look.

To make a label with fabric scraps

1. Cut two small pieces of fabric to the same shape, then sew up the sides and bottom edge.

2. Trim the seam allowance. Turn out and push out the corners. Press.

3. Sew into your seam as a tag.

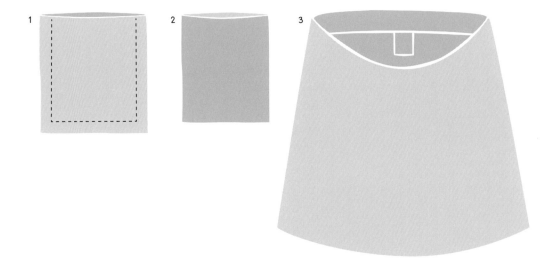

How to sew a hem

A hem is the finished edge of a garment that has been folded under and sewn so that it doesn't fray. There are many ways to finish hems, but my favourite go-to method is a double fold hem. Simply fold the raw edge over once and press, then fold over a second time and press again. Pin and then stitch a straight seam along the edge of the fold. You can also make a hem template as suggested In the casing tutorial (see page 64).

TIP

Never be afraid to reach out to the sewing community (or Google) for help. The internet is an excellent resource for how-to videos, product reviews and inspiration. If you don't know how to do something, chances are there will be blog posts or videos showing you many different ways to do that thing!

MAKE MAKE MAKE

DIY

DIY
STYLE

LOOK AFTER ME
Treat me with care
Use common sense
Wash only when dirty
Mend me if I break

SELF TAUGHT

How to care for your handmade creations

Once you have finished sewing up a handmade creation, you now have to take care of it to make sure it lasts you many wears and years to come.

Wash

Wash your handmade clothing when required using a short, gentle cycle and cool water. You can also handwash your me-mades if they are made from a delicate fabric.

Dry

Hang to dry on the washing line or a coat hanger. Air drying rather than tumble drying is gentler on your clothing and also saves energy.

Mend

Mending your me-mades can be just as rewarding as sewing up the garment the first time. There are lots of ways to visibly or invisibly mend clothing and extend its life.

Upcycle, gift or donate

When a me-made no longer fits or suits your style, you can upcycle it into something new, gift it to a friend or family member or donate it.

PART 2

Accessory Projects

Scrunchie

#diydaisyscrunchie

Scrunchies are gentle on hair, and I don't think they will ever go out of style. I love to match my scrunchie to my outfit – I have scrunchies in almost every colour. They are a great beginner project and scrap buster, and also make an excellent gift. Scrunchies forever!

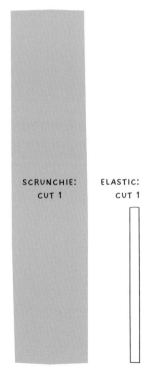

Scrunchie: cut 1

12 cm (4 ¾ in) x 60 cm (23 ½ in)

5–10 mm (¼–½ in) elastic: cut 1

Length = The circumference of your wrist + 2 cm (¾ in) or 20–22 cm (8–8 ¾ in)

1. Fold the rectangle in half with the right sides together and pin. Sew up the side seam, leaving a small gap about 3 cm (1 ¼ in) wide close to one end.

2. Turn the scrunchie tube right side out using a safety pin. Press.

3. Turn the shorter end of the tube and push it through the gap.

4. Insert the other end of the tube through the gap and align the ends of the tube. Sew around the raw edges of the two ends.

5. Pull the fabric out through the gap; your tube has now become a scrunchie loop. Thread the elastic through the loop using a safety pin, and secure the ends of the elastic with a tight knot or overlap and stitch together.

6. Sew the gap closed and snip loose threads.

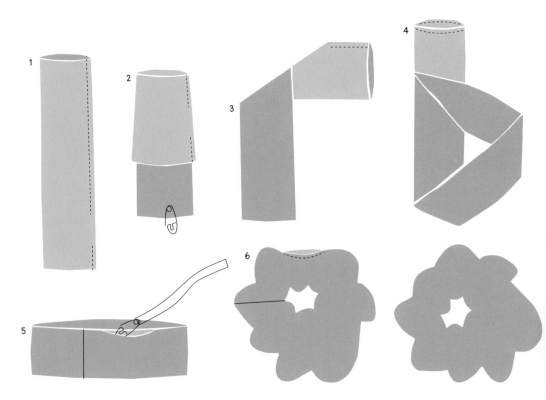

Tie Scrunchie

Add a tie to your scrunchie to use up remnants. It looks so cute! The Tie Scrunchie is pictured on page 35.

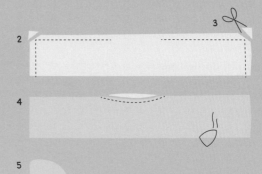

Scrunchie: cut 1

Use formula on page 79

5–10 mm (¼–½ in) elastic: cut 1

Use formula on page 79

Ribbon tie: cut 1

10 cm (4 in) x 40 cm (15 ¾ in)

1. Complete steps 1–6 of the Scrunchie opposite.

2. Fold the ribbon tie rectangle in half with right sides together and sew a seam on the three sides with raw edges, leaving a 5 cm (2 in) gap in the centre of the longest side.

3. Clip corners and trim excess seam allowance.

4. Turn the tie right side out through the gap and press. Stitch the gap closed and snip loose threads.

5. Tie the ribbon around the scrunchie in a knot or a bow.

Bandana

#diydaisybandana

Bandanas have so many uses and are a great project to practise sewing straight rolled hems. They also make a great two-in-one gift, doubling as gift wrap and an accessory. If you have a little piece of fabric left over from your latest creation, you could even sew up a mini version for a furry friend!

Bandana: cut 1

52 cm (20 ½ in) x 52 cm (20 ½ in)

BANDANA: CUT 1

1. Sew a straight stitch down the sides of the square 5 mm (¼ in) from the edge. Repeat on the top and bottom edges.

2. Fold the seam allowance with wrong sides facing and press it towards the centre of the square. Start with the sides and then press the top and bottom.

3. Trim the excess seam allowance and then fold the hem over again. Press in the same order: sides first, and then top and bottom edges.

4. Sew a straight stitch down the sides and then top and bottom. Trim any loose threads, fold in half along the diagonal with wrong sides touching, and your bandana is ready.

Variation

Triangle Top

When I was a kid, my twin sister and I spent many nights wrestling maths formulas at the dinner table with DIY Dad. When I was working out a formula for this project, I had to do the same – but there were no tears shed this time. Here is a formula that takes your measurements and gives you the square dimensions to make a Triangle Top to fit your chest perfectly, using the sewing method of the Bandana.

Triangle top: cut 1

Width and height = High bust x 0.7 + 10 cm (4 in)

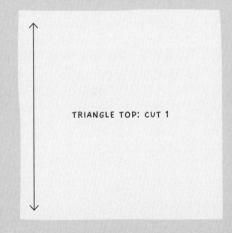

TRIANGLE TOP: CUT 1

Tote Bag

#diydaisytotebag

Always cute and handy, tote bags are a great beginner sewing project to practise straight seams. This tote includes other techniques used throughout the book, like sewing a facing, understitching and topstitching. Make it your own: add an inner or outer patch pocket to organise and separate your things (see page 70), scrunchify the straps (see page 96), or patchwork fabric together to use up your scraps. Tote bag too small? Increase the dimensions of the pattern pieces by 5 or 10 cm (2 or 4 in) for an extra oversized bag. As well as the fabric suggestions on pages 30–31, this also works in heavier fabrics like denim and canvas. Both the Tote Bag and Scrunchie Strap Bag (see page 96) pictured here have been made with second-hand fabric!

PATTERN PIECES

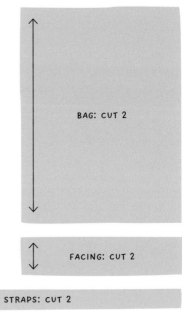

BAG: CUT 2

FACING: CUT 2

STRAPS: CUT 2

Bag: cut 2
40 cm (15 ¾ in) x 45 cm (17 ¾ in)

Straps: cut 2
8 cm (3 ¼ in) x 70 cm (27 ½ in)

Facing: cut 2
40 cm (15 ¾ in) x 10 cm (4 in)

1. On the right side of the fabric, mark the strap placement on the top edge of each bag rectangle, 12 cm (4 ¾ in) in from each side.

2. Next sew the straps. Fold each strap in half lengthways with the right sides together and pin. Sew a side seam along each strap, then turn out using a safety pin and iron flat. Topstitch along each edge.

3. Match the straps to the marks on the top edge of each bag rectangle, aligning the raw ends of the straps with the raw edge of the bag. Pin and then stitch in place using a 5 mm (¼ in) seam allowance.

4. Place the bag rectangles together with right sides facing and sew up the side and bottom seams. If the straps are getting in the way, pin them to the centre of each rectangle. Turn the bag right side out and set aside.

5. Now place the facing rectangles together with right sides facing and sew up the side seams. Press the seams open. Press a 1 cm (½ in) single fold hem with wrong sides facing along the bottom edge of the facing.

6. Slide the facing around the top of the bag so that right sides are together and you're sandwiching the straps between bag and facing. Align the side seams and the top edges, pin and then sew around the top edge with a 1½ cm (½ in) seam allowance.

7. Turn the bag inside out and tuck the straps into the bag (if they're not already pinned). Press the seam allowance towards the facing.

8. Understitch the seam allowance to the facing to stop it from rolling out.

9. Fold the facing down over the bag, press and topstitch along the bottom edge of the facing to secure it to the bag and enclose all the raw edges. Pull the straps out of the bag before sewing this seam so you don't sew over them.

10. Turn the bag right side out, snip loose threads and press.

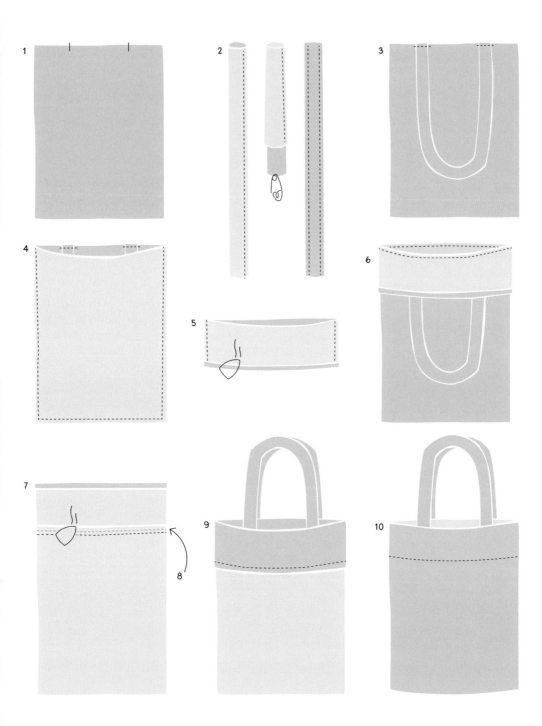

Variation

Ruffle Tote

Take a tote from simple to wowza with the addition of a ruffle. The technique used to create a ruffle is gathering, and it can be used to jazz up every project in this book. No project will go unruffled! The Ruffle Tote is pictured on page 92.

PATTERN PIECES

Bag: cut 2

40 cm (15 ¾ in) x 45 cm (17 ¾ in)

Straps: cut 2

8 cm (3 ¼ in) x 70 cm (27 ½ in)

Facing: cut 2

40 cm (15 ¾ in) x 10 cm (4 in)

Ruffle: cut 1

20 cm (8 in) x 195 cm (76 ¾ in)

BAG: CUT 2

FACING: CUT 2

STRAPS: CUT 2

RUFFLE: CUT 1

1. Complete steps 1–3 of the Tote Bag (see page 88).

2. Fold the ruffle right sides together and sew the ends. Turn right side out and press. Mark the centre of the ruffle along the raw edge – this will be the top edge of the ruffle.

3. On one tote rectangle, mark the centre along the bottom edge. Mark 12 cm (4 ¾ in) down from the top of the tote bag on both sides.

4. Make the ruffle, gathering the top edge (see page 52). The finished ruffle length should be about 105 cm (41 ¼ in).

5. Right sides together, align the centre mark on the ruffle with the centre mark on the tote rectangle and pin. Match the ends of the ruffle to the marks you made 12 cm (4 ¾ in) down on each side of the tote and pin. Spread the gathers evenly along the sides and bottom of the rectangle and then pin in place. Press. Stitch the gathers to the tote rectangle using a long stitch length and a 5 mm (¼ in) seam allowance.

6. Complete the bag using steps 4–10 of the Tote Bag.

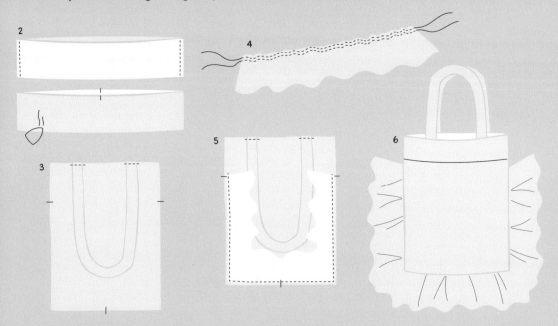

Pocket Bag

#diydaisypocketbag

When I first started sewing I was afraid to sew in-seam pockets, but without them my hands were often full – and so I created the Pocket Bag. On the one hand, it was an excuse to make another accessory, and on the other, it was super helpful for holding my important pocket-holding things. This is a great project to help you practise sewing French seams (see page 49). As well as the fabric suggestions on pages 30–31, this also works in heavier fabrics like denim and canvas.

PATTERN PIECES

Strap: cut 1

10 cm (4 in) x 120 cm (47 ¼ in)

Bag: cut 1

25 cm (10 in) x 50 cm (19 ¾ in)

Facing: cut 2

25 cm (10 in) x 6 cm (2 ½ in)

BAG: CUT 1

FACING: CUT 2

STRAP: CUT 1

1. Sew the strap by completing steps 1–5 of the Tie Belt (see page 100). Edgestitch along the sides of the strap.

2. Fold the bag rectangle in half with wrong sides facing and sew up the sides with a 5 mm (¼ in) seam allowance. Trim 2 mm (⅛ in) from the seam allowance, turn the bag wrong side out and press the seams flat. Then sew up the side seams with a 5 mm (¼ in) seam allowance. Turn the bag right side out, press and set aside.

3. Place facing rectangles together with wrong sides facing and sew up the side seams with a 5 mm (¼ in) seam allowance. Trim 2 mm (⅛ in) from the seam allowance, turn the facing wrong side out and press the seams flat. Then sew up the side seams with a 5 mm (¼ in) seam allowance. Press a 1 cm (½ in) single fold hem with wrong sides facing along the bottom edge of the facing.

4. Take the bag and, on the right side of the fabric, pin each end of the strap to a side seam, aligning the raw ends of the strap with the raw edge of the bag. Stitch in place with a 5 mm (¼ in) seam allowance.

5. Slide the facing around the top of the bag so that right sides are together and you're sandwiching the straps between bag and facing. Align the side seams and the top edges, pin and then sew around the top edge with a 1 cm (½ in) seam allowance.

6. Turn the bag inside out and tuck the strap into the bag. Press the seam allowance towards the facing.

7. Understitch the seam allowance to the facing to stop it from rolling out.

8. Fold the facing down over the bag, press and topstitch along the bottom edge of the facing to secure it to the bag. Pull the strap out of the bag before sewing this seam so you don't sew over it.

9. Turn the bag right side out, snip loose threads and press.

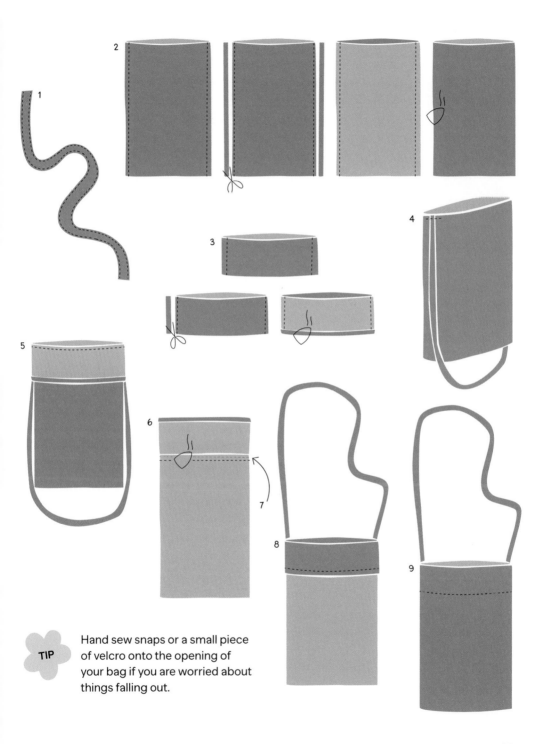

1

2

3

4

5

6

7

8

9

TIP Hand sew snaps or a small piece of velcro onto the opening of your bag if you are worried about things falling out.

Variation

Scrunchie Strap Bag

Hack the strap on the Pocket Bag by making it scrunchie. If your fabric is opaque (not see-through), your inner straps could be made out of scrap fabric as they won't be visible on the outside. A great scrap buster! The Scrunchie Strap Bag is pictured on page 86.

PATTERN PIECES

Inner strap: cut 1

10 cm (4 in) x 120 cm (47 ¼ in)

Scrunchie strap: cut 1

8 cm (3 ¼ in) x 180 cm (70 ¾ in)

Bag: cut 1

25 cm (10 in) x 50 cm (19 ¾ in)

Facing: cut 2

25 cm (10 in) x 6 cm (2 ½ in)

TIP

Create the scrunchie look for straps of almost any size or length on any garment or accessory! First get your inner strap sewn and ready to attach. Then use this formula to cut out two rectangles for the scrunchie tube:

Width = Finished inner strap width x 2 + 3 cm (1 ¼ in)

Length = Finished inner strap length x 1.5

Then complete your scrunchie strap by following steps 2–6 of the Scrunchie Strap Bag.

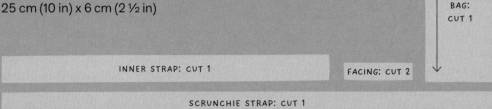

INNER STRAP: CUT 1

FACING: CUT 2

BAG: CUT 1

SCRUNCHIE STRAP: CUT 1

1. Sew the inner strap by completing steps 1–6 of the Tie Belt (see page 100).

2. Fold the scrunchie rectangle in half with right sides together and pin. Sew up the edge with a 1 cm (½ in) seam allowance to create a tube.

3. Pin a large safety pin to one end of the tube. Insert the head of the safety pin inside the tube and thread it through to the other end. As you pull on the safety pin, you will pull the tube right side out. Press.

4. Pin the safety pin to one end of the inner strap. Insert the pin's head into the outer strap and thread it through, bunching up the outer strap as you go. Pin the other end of the inner strap to the end of the outer strap to stop the inner strap from threading all the way through. Stitch these ends together to secure.

5. After threading the safety pin out the end, pin the ends together and stitch to secure. Make sure the inner strap isn't twisted before stitching the end.

6. Spread the outer strap evenly and press flat. Pin along the strap every 10–15 cm (4–6 in) and sew little lines about 3–5 stitches long where the pins are to keep the scrunches even. Snip loose threads.

7. Complete steps 2–9 of the Pocket Bag (see page 94).

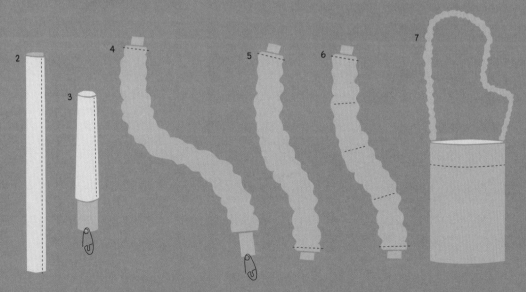

Tie Belt

#diydaisytiebelt

You never know when a tie belt will come in handy! Part of this construction process is used a couple of times in the book, so I break it down here so you can refer back to it later. When I make a dress, I usually sew a tie belt in the leftover fabric so I have one that matches.

Tie belt: cut 1

Width = Waist x 2 + 3 cm (1 ¼ in)

Height = 16 cm (6 ¼ in)

TIE BELT: CUT 1

1. Fold the rectangle in half with the wrong sides facing and press.

2. Open it up and fold each edge to the centre line with the wrong sides facing. Press.

3. Fold the belt in half, so the small folds are right sides together. Press.

4. Open everything back out and fold in half with the right sides together. Pin each end, matching up the creases made in the previous steps. Sew the ends and trim the seam allowance.

5. Turn right side out and fold the raw edges back into the belt. Press.

6. Edgestitch along the sides and ends to finish the belt.

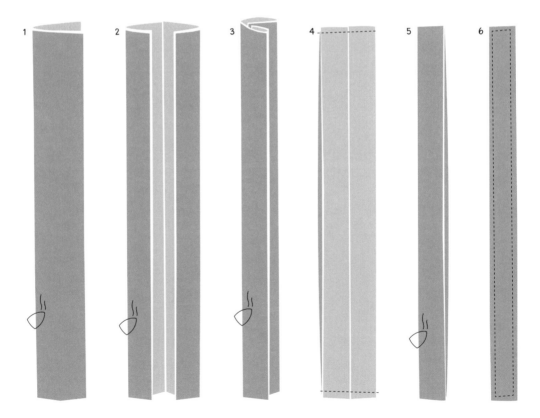

Hair Scarf

With a few adjustments of the dimensions (and the same sewing method), the Tie Belt can become a Hair Scarf! Pictured on page 45.

Hair scarf: cut 1

Width = Circumference of your head x 3

Height = 14 cm (5 ½ in)

HAIR SCARF: CUT 1

Scrunchie Headband

#diydaisyscrunchieheadband

Have you ever worn a croissant on your head? No? Me neither, but a Scrunchie Headband comes pretty close. If you want some scrunchie action but your hair is too short, this is for you! Sew one up to match an outfit or make a set to wear at a party. The Scrunchie Headband is also a fun project to sew with friends – hens' party or baby shower activity sorted!

1 padded ribbon-wrapped or fabric-covered headband (it needs to be ribbon-wrapped or fabric-covered so you can stitch into it)

Hand-sewing needle

Scrunchie: cut 1

20 cm (8 in) x 80 cm (31 ½ in)

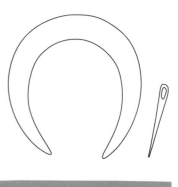

SCRUNCHIE: CUT 1

1. Fold the rectangle in half with right sides facing and sew up the long edge to make a tube.

2. Press the seam open. Sew up one end and then sew the other only halfway, leaving a hole big enough to fit the headband through.

3. Turn the tube right side out and press.

4. Insert the headband through the hole.

5. Fold the corners over each other and hand sew together, catching the headband with the stitches. This will prevent the fabric from slipping off the headband. Repeat on the other end of the headband and snip loose threads.

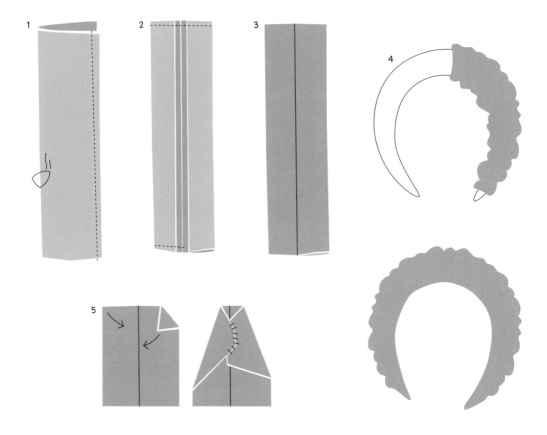

Two-Tone Mini Headband

Want something a little smaller and more colourful? Use the formulas below to measure your headband and make something less full and ruffly but with an extra colour — perfect for using small remnants and double the cuteness! The Two-Tone Mini Headband is pictured on page 102.

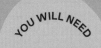

YOU WILL NEED

1 regular ribbon-wrapped or fabric-covered headband

Hand-sewing needle

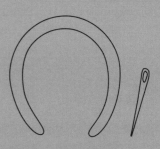

SCRUNCHIE: CUT 1, COLOUR 1 SCRUNCHIE: CUT 1, COLOUR 2

PATTERN PIECES

Scrunchie: cut 1 in each colour

Width = Length of headband x 1.5 + 2 cm (¾ in) ÷ 2

Height = Circumference of headband x 2 + 2 cm (¾ in)

1. Place the rectangles together with right sides facing and sew along one short edge to make one scrunchie piece. Press the center seam open, and then complete steps 1–5 of the Scrunchie Headband opposite.

Face Mask

#diydaisyfacemask

Masks aren't *just* worn for protection anymore; they have become a fashion accessory that you can match with your outfit. These two-layer masks can be worn over a disposable mask for extra protection. I have made a bunch of these for my family and always keep one handy in my tote bag in case I need one. Don't forget to wash them after each wear! I prefer to make face masks in cotton – either poplin or lawn.

Mask: cut 2

24 cm (9 ½ in) x 20 cm (8 in)

Elastic: cut 2

5–10 mm (¼–½ in) x 40 cm (15 ¾ in)

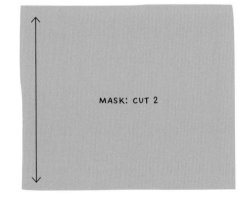

MASK: CUT 2

ELASTIC: CUT 2

1. Place the rectangles with right sides facing and sew the top and bottom seams.

2. Turn the fabric right side out and iron the seams flat. Topstitch along the top and bottom edge.

3. Fold three evenly spaced pleats, all in the same direction, and press them flat. They will be pointing down when the mask is finished. Sew a straight stitch down both sides to secure the pleats.

4. Create a small casing on the side of the mask with a 1 cm (½ in) double fold. Mark a line 2 cm (¾ in) from the side and fold the edge to this line. Press, then fold again. Sew a straight stitch along the edge of the casing, making sure to backstitch.

5. Using a safety pin, thread the ear-loop elastic through the casing.

6. Secure the elastic with a loose knot. Tighten the knot when you are comfortable with the fit of the ear loops. Snip any loose threads.

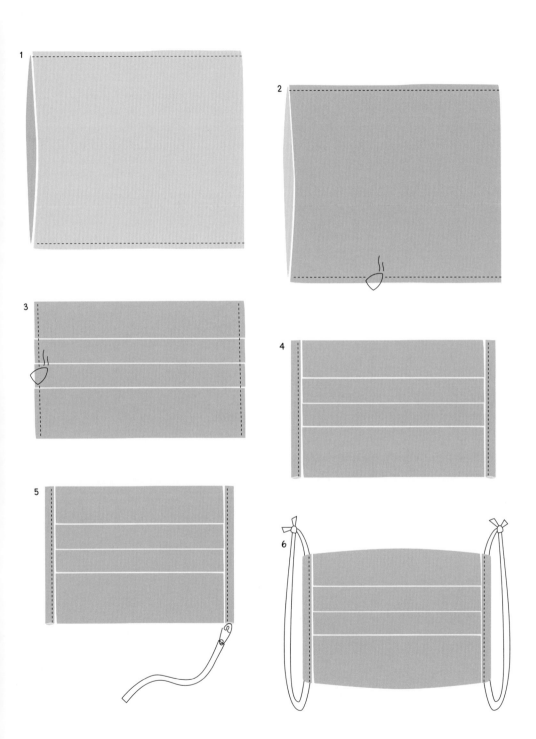

Variation

Bias Binding
Face Mask

Not a fan of elastic around your ears? Use bias binding instead. The perfect opportunity for some colour blocking.

Mask: cut 2

20 cm (8 in) x 20 cm (8 in)

Double fold bias binding for tie: cut 2

Length = 70 cm (27 ½ in)

1. Complete steps 1–3 of the Face Mask (see page 108).

2. Mark the centre of one length of bias binding and align it with the centre of the mask along the side. Pin the binding to the mask, sandwiching the raw edges between the binding. Sew along the edge of the binding to secure it to the mask. Repeat with the second piece of binding. Snip any loose threads and try it on!

Cross-Back Apron

#diydaisyapron

I'm a pretty clumsy cook, so I usually wear an apron to protect my outfits, especially if they are me-mades. I often wear an apron when I'm sewing too. If, like mine, your apron will get a lot of wear and be washed frequently, it's best to choose a sturdy fabric, like midweight or heavyweight linen, denim, canvas or cotton twill. Add patch pockets in any size you like to keep your tools handy. I've always got a safety pin, spool of thread or piece of chalk in mine!

Straps: cut 2

Width = 12 cm (4 ¾ in)

Length = Top of shoulder to under bust x 2

Apron: cut 1

Width = Full bust + 15 cm (6 in)

Height = High bust to knees or desired length

Facing: cut 1

Width = Full bust + 15 cm (6 in)

Height = 12 cm (4 ¾ in)

1. For midweight fabrics, sew two straps using the method in step 2 of the Tote Bag (see page 88). For heavyweight fabrics, use the Tie Belt method (see page 100); however, instead of folding the outer edges all the way to the centre (as in step 2 of that method), fold them in by 1 cm (½ in).

2. Sew a 1 cm (½ in) double fold hem (see page 73) on the sides and bottom edge of the apron rectangle. Then sew a 1 cm (½ in) double fold hem on the sides of the facing, and press a 1 cm (½ in) single fold hem along the bottom edge (wrong sides together).

3. Mark the centre front of the apron rectangle. Measure from the centre of your chest out to where you'd like the straps to sit, and then mark this measurement on the fabric on both sides.

4. On the right side of the fabric, put the straps on the marks you made in step 3, aligning the raw ends of the straps with the raw edge of the apron. Pin and then sew the front straps to the apron with a 5 mm (¼ in) seam allowance.

5. Pin the other ends of the straps to the diagonally opposite corners of the apron, again aligning the raw edges. Try on the apron to test the strap length and shorten if required. When you have found the length you'd like, stitch the straps in place at the back using a 5 mm (¼ in) seam allowance.

6. Lay the facing onto the apron with right sides together, sandwiching the straps between the apron and facing. Pin in place and then sew along the top edge with a 1 cm (½ in) seam allowance.

7. Open out the facing and press the seam allowance up. Understitch the seam allowance to the facing to stop it from rolling out when the apron is worn. Make sure the straps are out of the way so you don't sew over them.

8. Fold the facing down so that the wrong sides of apron and facing are together and press. Topstitch along the bottom edge of the facing to secure it to the apron and enclose all the raw edges, then snip loose threads.

Variation

Apron Crop

This apron variation isn't exactly an accessory but it's a great piece to wear layered with your other creations. You can even wear it alone as a cute crop top with an open back. The sewing method is the same as the Cross-Back Apron; all you need to do is adjust the pattern pieces. I've also added scrunchie straps to the one pictured here, using the method on page 97.

PATTERN PIECES

Straps: cut 2

Width = 12 cm (4 ¾ in)

Length = Top of shoulder to under bust x 2

Apron: cut 1

Width = Full bust + 15 cm (6 in)

Height = High bust to belly button

Facing: cut 1

Width = Full bust + 15 cm (6 in)

Height = 12 cm (4 ¾ in)

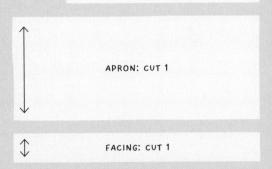

Gathered Collar

#diydaisygatheredcollar

Sometimes an outfit needs something extra to take it to the next level, and that something could just be a detachable collar. My favourite way to style a collar is over a plain boxy t-shirt worn with a Sophie Trapezoid Skirt (see page 139). This collar creation is a great way to practise skills like gathering, applying bias binding and sewing a straight stitch – and it's so simple and easy to sew, you might end up making one for every day of the week!

Collar: cut 1

40 cm (15 ¾ in) x 120 cm (47 ¼ in)

Double fold bias binding for tie: cut 1

Length = 1 m (1 ⅛ yd)

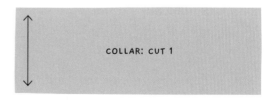

COLLAR: CUT 1

BIAS BINDING TIE: CUT 1

1. Fold the rectangle in half lengthways with right sides together and sew up the short sides. Turn out and press.

2. Mark the centre of the collar rectangle and the centre of the bias binding.

3. Gather the raw edge of the collar (see page 52). The finished length should be 60–70 cm (23 ½–27 ½ in), depending on how wide you'd like the neck hole to be. Spread the gathers evenly and place it around your neck to test the fit, adjusting if necessary.

4. Align the centre marks on the bias binding and collar. Bind the neckline with bias binding using the sandwich method (see page 59).

5. Tie a small knot at each end of the binding to keep it from unravelling. Snip any loose threads and press.

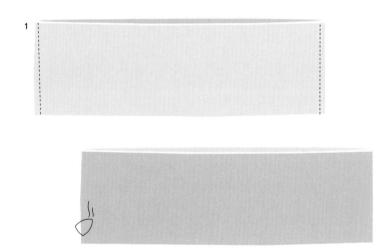

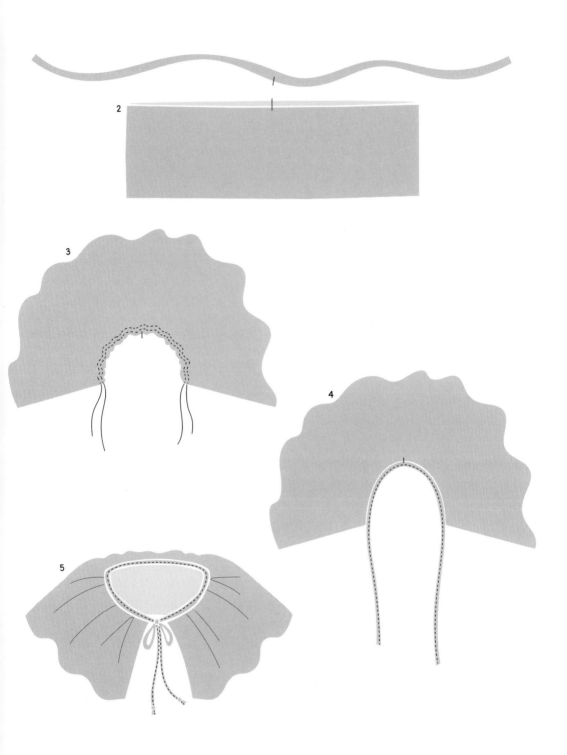

Rectangle Collar

This is reminiscent of a sailor collar and looks very quirky layered over other garments. You can also curve the edges for a more classic look. The Rectangle Collar is pictured on page 168.

PATTERN PIECES

Collar: cut 2

60 cm (23 ½ in) x 40 cm (15 ¾ in)

Double fold bias binding for tie: cut 1

Length = 100 cm (39 ¼ in)

TEMPLATE

Neckline template (see page 62)

BIAS BINDING
TIE: CUT 1

COLLAR: CUT 2

1. Fold one rectangle in half widthways with right sides together. Place the back neckline template 15 cm (6 in) from the top edge, aligning the centre back with the fold. Trace the template and then use a ruler to continue the line parallel with the fold down to the bottom edge.

2. Cut out to create the neckline, then lay the collar on the second rectangle. Trace the neckline and cut to create a second identical pattern piece.

3. Put the collar rectangles together with right sides facing. Sew around the outside edges, leaving the neck hole open. Clip the corners and trim the seam allowance to reduce bulk.

4. Turn out the collar and press. Mark the centre back of the neck opening and the centre of the bias binding. Align the centre marks and attach the bias binding to the neckline using the sandwich method (see page 59). Snip any loose threads and press.

Button Earrings

#diydaisybuttonearrings

I know I said no buttons are used in this book, but take a look at these ear adornments and tell me they aren't cute! These earrings are so satisfying to make because they use up some of your smaller scraps – and who doesn't like matching their earrings to their outfit? You can also create fabric-covered buttons to match your future me-makes that might use them!

YOU WILL NEED

Button-covering kit
(you can find these at most craft stores and some dollar shops)

Fabric scraps

Needle nose or blunt nose pliers

Super glue or E-6000 craft glue

Earring backs: posts or clip-ons

1. Follow the kit's instructions to make a pair of fabric-covered buttons using your fabric scraps.

2. Squeeze the loop on the back of the button with the pliers and gently wiggle it out of the button.

3. Squirt a small blob of glue onto the back of the button and then stick it on the earring back. Repeat so that you have a pair of earrings. Leave them for about 15–20 minutes or until the glue is dry before wearing them.

Variation

Barrettes

I used to wear fabric hair accessories a lot when I was a teenager and I don't know why I forgot about them! They look SUPER sweet. This is a quick no-sew project – time to get out that hot glue gun!

YOU WILL NEED

Felt or thin batting

Hair clip barrettes
(the ones with plastic on
top of the clip work best)

Hot glue gun and glue

Fabric scraps

1. Cut out a strip of felt or batting, the same size as the plastic top of the barrette, and hot glue it on top to provide some padding.

2. Place the barrette on the wrong side of the fabric and trace around the edges, adding a 1 cm (½ in) allowance on all sides. Cut out the fabric.

3. Lay the fabric right side down and then place the barrette right side down on top of the fabric. Apply some hot glue around the edge of the fabric and then fold it over onto the underside of the plastic, pressing down carefully. Be sure not to glue the clip part. Do this all the way around the edges, making sure the fabric is taut. Leave them for about 15–20 minutes or until the glue is dry before trying them on.

PART 3

Clothing Projects

Stephanie Rectangle-Sleeve Top

#diystephanietop

This rectangle-sleeve top was my first introduction to minimal or zero waste sewing. I was buying expensive fabric but didn't want to waste an inch, so I played around with rectangles, utilising the full width of the fabric. The result was a simple boxy top that looks great with jeans or a Sonya Ruffle Skirt (see page 177). Because we are all different sizes, using the full width of the fabric won't work for everyone – here's my formula to make this top in any size.

Top: cut 2

Width = Arm bust ÷ 2 (includes ease) + 2 cm (¾ in)

Height = Top of shoulder to desired length (waist or hip) + 2 cm (¾ in)

Sleeves: cut 2

Width = Arm bust ÷ 2 + 2 cm (¾ in)

Height = Edge of shoulder to elbow or desired length + 2 cm (¾ in)

Double fold bias binding for neckline: cut 1

Length = As long as neck opening

Neckline template (see page 62)

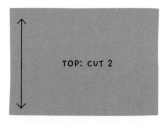

TOP: CUT 2

SLEEVES: CUT 2

NECKLINE BIAS BINDING: CUT 1

1. Fold each of the top rectangles in half widthways with the right sides together and the fold to the left. Place the front neckline template in the top left corner of one of the rectangles, aligning the centre with the fold. Trace and cut out the neck hole. Repeat for the back neckline on the second rectangle.

2. Place the top rectangles together with right sides facing. Pin and then sew one shoulder seam.

3. Bind the neckline with bias binding using the sandwich method or facing method (see pages 59 or 60).

4. Put the top rectangles together again with right sides facing. Pin and then sew the other shoulder seam.

5. Mark the centre of both sleeve rectangles on the edge of the sleeve that you will attach to the top.

6. With the right sides of the fabric together, align the centre mark on one of the sleeve rectangles to a shoulder seam and pin it along the edge of the top. Sew the sleeve onto the top. Repeat on the other side with the second sleeve.

7. Fold the top from the shoulder seams so that the right sides are facing and align the edges of the top and underarms of the sleeves. Pin and sew the side seams of the top and the underarm seams of the sleeves. Clip into the seam allowance at the corners if required to reduce bulk, making sure not to snip the stitching.

8. Hem the sleeves and bottom of the top (see page 73). Snip any loose threads and press.

Variation

Rectangle-Sleeve Jacket

When I'm wearing my big-sleeve creations, sometimes the only thing that will fit over the top is a Rectangle-Sleeve Jacket. Cropped and comfy, this boxy jacket will look great with your DIY outfits. This jacket is best in a fabric that keeps its shape, such as cotton lawn or poplin, midweight or heavyweight linen, denim or canvas.

PATTERN PIECES

Jacket: cut 2

Width = Arm bust ÷ 2 (includes ease) + 2 cm (¾ in)

Height = Top of shoulder to hip + 2 cm (¾ in)

Sleeves: cut 2

Width = Arm bust ÷ 2 + 2 cm (¾ in)

Height = Edge of shoulder to elbow or desired length + 2 cm (¾ in)

Double fold bias binding for neckline: cut 1

Length = As long as jacket opening + 10 cm (4 in)

NECKLINE BIAS BINDING: CUT 1 ▬▬▬▬▬▬▬▬▬▬▬▬▬▬▬▬▬▬

TEMPLATE

Neckline template (see page 62)

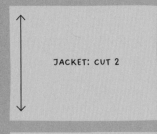

JACKET: CUT 2

SLEEVES: CUT 2

1. Fold each of the jacket rectangles in half widthways and follow step 1 of the Stephanie Rectangle-Sleeve Top (see page 132).

2. Put the back piece aside, and with the jacket front still folded in half, mark a straight line from the edge of the neck hole to the bottom corner of the rectangle. Cut along the line to turn the jacket front into two pieces.

3. Place the front pieces onto the jacket back with the right sides together. Pin and then sew the shoulder seams.

4. Mark the centre of both sleeve rectangles on the edge of the sleeve that you will attach to the jacket. With the right sides together, align the centre mark on one of the sleeve rectangles to a shoulder seam and pin it along the edge of the jacket. Sew the sleeve onto the jacket. Repeat with the second sleeve.

5. Fold the jacket from the shoulder seams so that the right sides are facing and align the edges of the jacket and the underarms of the sleeves. Pin and sew the side seams of the jacket and the underarm seams of the sleeves. You can sew the underarm with a curve and clip into the allowance to reduce bulk under the arm.

6. Hem the sleeves and bottom of the jacket (see page 73).

7. Measure the length of the jacket opening and add 10 cm (4 in). Cut a piece of bias binding to the length required, or make your own (see page 56).

8. Mark the centre of the binding and the centre of the opening on the back of the jacket. Align the centre marks and pin the binding to the raw edge of the jacket opening all the way around. Sew the binding onto the jacket using the sandwich method (see page 59). Tie a small knot at each end of the binding to keep it from unravelling. The tails of the binding will hang down the front of the jacket as a design feature. Snip any loose threads and press.

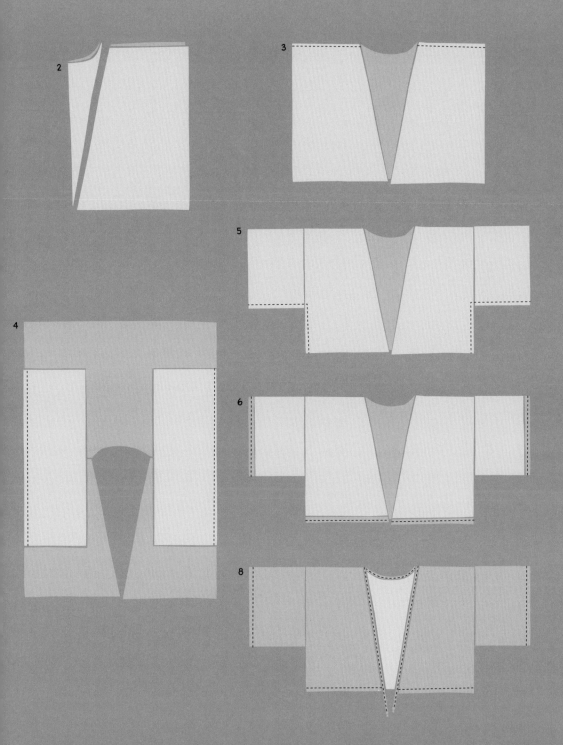

Sophie Trapezoid Skirt

#diysophieskirt

When I lived in Tokyo, I embraced uniform dressing and started to really define my sewing style – simple, ruffled, colourful. I made this skirt in a bunch of colours so I could rotate them throughout the week to wear at work, while exploring the countryside by bike, or sitting under cherry blossoms enjoying a picnic in the park. Depending on the width of your fabric and your measurements, you may need to cut your skirt pieces as halves; this will mean that as well as side seams, there will be a centre front and centre back seam.

PATTERN PIECES

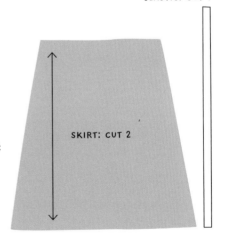

ELASTIC: CUT 1

SKIRT: CUT 2

Skirt: cut 2

Width at waist = Hips at widest point ÷ 2 + 20 cm (8 in) + 2 cm (¾ in)

Width at hem = Hips at widest point ÷ 2 + 40 cm (15 ¾ in) + 2 cm (¾ in)

Height = Waist to desired length + (width of elastic x 2 + 1 cm/½ in) + 2 cm (¾ in)

2 ½ cm (1 in) non-roll elastic for waistband: cut 1

Length = Waist − 10 cm (4 in)

1. With the right sides facing, place the skirt front and back together. Pin and sew the side seams.

2. Sew a waistband casing (see page 64). Begin by matching up the side seams and pinning them together, and then pin along the rest of the waistband. If there's a little bit of excess fabric when pinning, just bunch it up and ease it into the waistband. When the skirt is finished you won't notice because the elastic inside the waistband will bunch it up even more.

3. After inserting the elastic into the casing, pin the ends together with a safety pin and try on the skirt to check the fit. Shorten the elastic if you'd like it a bit tighter. When you're happy with the fit, stitch the ends of the elastic together to secure them before you close up the casing.

4. Hem the bottom of the skirt (see page 73). Snip loose threads and press.

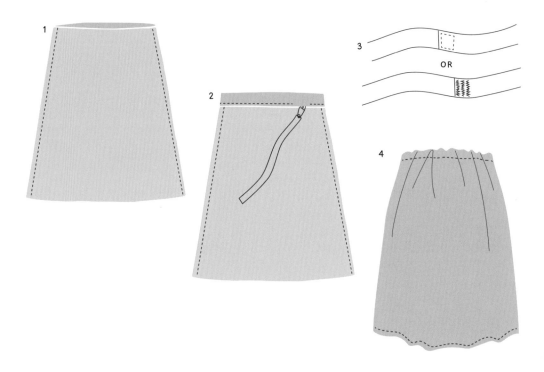

Two-Tone Skirt

This is my Yin and Yang skirt: take two different colours or even prints (florals and ginghams, I'm looking at you) and mix them together for a bold statement piece. You can apply this method to any of your creations – splice it up, baby!

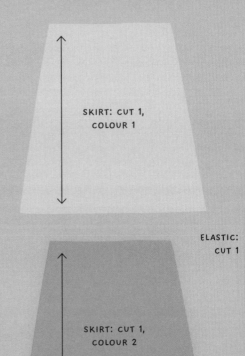

SKIRT: CUT 1, COLOUR 1

SKIRT: CUT 1, COLOUR 2

ELASTIC: CUT 1

PATTERN PIECES

Skirt: cut 1 in each colour

Use skirt formula on page 139

2 ½ cm (1 in) non-roll elastic for waistband: cut 1

Length = Waist – 10 cm (4 in)

1. Place the trapezoids together with right sides facing up on both pieces. Mark a curvy line on the top trapezoid with chalk and then cut through both pieces at the same time. You will end up with four pieces of fabric, two in each colour.

2. Staystitch along all four curved edges to stop the fabric from stretching. Set your stitch length to 1 ½ mm (¹⁄₁₆ in) and sew along the curved edges with a 5 mm (¼ in) seam allowance. Let the presser foot move the fabric through the machine to ensure you don't stretch or pull the fabric as you sew.

3. Pin the curved edges with right sides together to their other halves in the contrasting colour. Sew up the curves with a 1 cm (½ in) seam allowance. Clip or notch the seam allowance if required to help the seams lie flat (see page 51), making sure not to clip into the stitches. Press the seams open.

4. Complete steps 1–4 of the Sophie Trapezoid Skirt (see page 140).

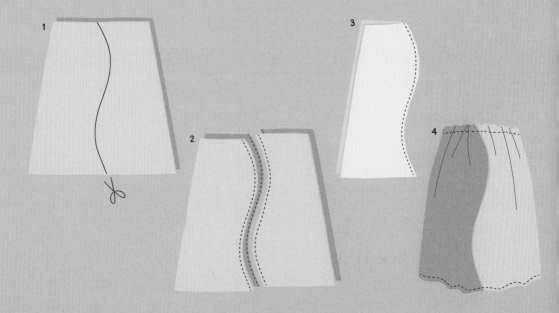

Hollie High-Neck Top

#diyhollietop

The classic pillowcase dress was one of my first DIY projects as a teenager, and I would also make tops similar to this one by upcycling floral shirts I found at op shops. Pillowcases don't fit every body, so I worked out a formula to make this in your size.

PATTERN PIECES

Top: cut 2

Width = Body measurement at widest point (hips, bust or tummy) ÷ 2 + 20 (8 in) cm

Height = Top of shoulder to desired length + 2 cm (¾ in)

Armhole height (A) = Top of shoulder to full bust

Neckline width (N) = Full bust ÷ 2

Double fold bias binding for neckline: cut 2

Length = Full bust ÷ 4 – 5 cm (2 in)

Double fold bias binding for armholes and straps: cut 2

Length = Armhole height (A) x 4

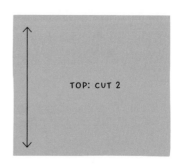

TOP: CUT 2

NECKLINE BIAS BINDING: CUT 2

STRAP BIAS BINDING: CUT 2

1. Fold one rectangle in half with the right sides together. Measuring from the top corner, mark the measurement for (A) down the side with the raw edges. Divide (N) by two – because the fabric is folded you need to halve this measurement – and mark this along the top edge, measuring across from the fold. Join the marks using a ruler and then cut along the line to create the armhole. Repeat with the second rectangle.

2. Place the pattern pieces together with right sides facing and sew up the side seams.

3. Gather the neckline edge on the front and back of the top (see page 52). The finished width should be the same as the neck binding. Press.

4. Bind the gathered edge of the neckline with the neck binding using the sandwich method (see page 59) and press.

5. Mark the centre of each length of the binding for the armholes and straps. Take one piece and match up the centre mark to a side seam and pin. Then pin the rest of the binding to the edge of the armhole. Sew the binding to the armhole, starting at one end of the binding and sewing around the armhole all the way to the other end. Tie each end of the binding into a tiny knot. Repeat with the other armhole.

6. Hem the bottom of the top (see page 73), snip loose threads and press. Tie the binding together to form straps.

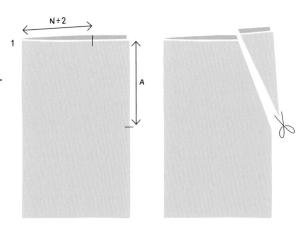

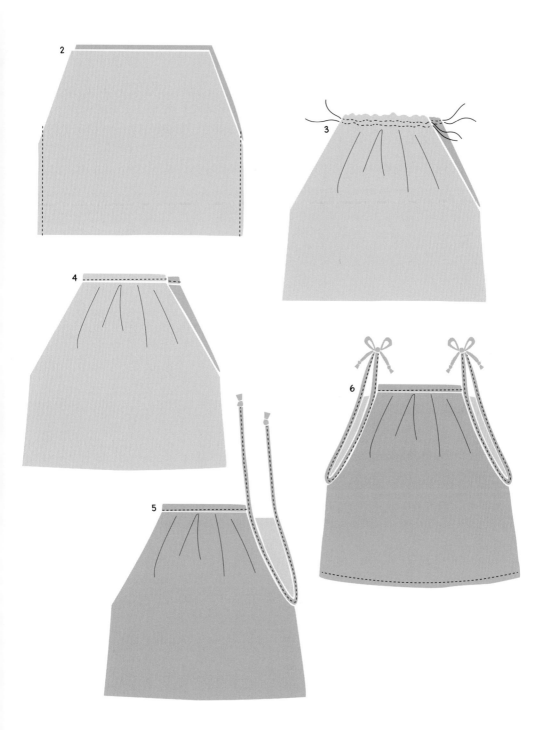

Variation

Asymmetric
Ruffle Dress

I add ruffles to almost all of my creations, because why not? You can never have enough ruffles!

PATTERN PIECES

Dress: cut 2

Use top formula on page 145

Ruffles: cut 4

Width = Dress width x 1.5

Height = 10 cm (4 in) + 2 cm (¾ in)

Double fold bias binding for neckline: cut 2

Length = Full bust ÷ 4 – 5 cm (2 in)

Double fold bias binding for armholes and straps: cut 1

Length = Armhole height x 4

DRESS: CUT 2

RUFFLES: CUT 4

NECKLINE BINDING: CUT 2

STRAP BIAS BINDING: CUT 2

1. Place two ruffle rectangles with right sides together and sew the side seams to make a loop. Hem the bottom edge (see page 73). Mark the centre front and back of the ruffle loop, then gather the raw edge (see page 52). Repeat with the other ruffle rectangles.

2. Sew the dress by completing steps 1–6 of the Hollie High-Neck Top (see page 146). Draw two asymmetric lines across the dress, making sure the topmost line is at least 5 cm (2 in) below the bottom of the armholes. Cut along the lines, so the dress is in three pieces. Mark the centre front and back on each piece, and mark the top edge of the middle piece.

3. Take one gathered ruffle loop and the top piece of the dress. With right sides facing, align the side seams of the ruffle and dress and pin. Match the centre front and back of the dress to the marks on the ruffle loop and pin. Spread the gathers evenly so that the circumference of the ruffle loop is the same as the dress. Pin and then stitch around the dress to attach the ruffle.

4. Press the ruffle flat and slide the middle piece of the dress, wrong side out, over the ruffle, sandwiching the ruffle in between the top and middle pieces of the dress. Align the edges and side seams and pin around the dress. Sew to attach and then pull the second piece of the dress and the ruffle down to press.

5. Repeat steps 3 and 4 with the second ruffle and bottom piece of the dress. Snip loose threads and press.

Kama Square-Neck Top

#diykamatop

With so many round-neck options in the book, I want to share another way to piece together rectangles and get a cool, wearable result. Instead of cutting out a neckline, you create it by placing the sleeves over the bodice and topstitching the two together. Play around with colour-blocked rectangles, or piece together vintage scarves to make your top even more unique.

Top: cut 2

Width = Full bust ÷ 2 + 10 cm (4 in) + 2 cm (¾ in)

Height = High bust to hip (this includes hem allowance, so finished length will be around the belly button)

Sleeves: cut 2

Width = Top of shoulder to full bust x 2 + 2 cm (¾ in)

Height = Edge of shoulder to elbow + 2 cm (¾ in)

TOP: CUT 2

SLEEVES: CUT 2

1. Hem the top edges of the top rectangles with a 1 cm (½ in) double fold hem (see page 73).

2. Hem three edges of the sleeve rectangles, starting with the sides and followed by the top edge, with a 1 cm (½ in) double fold hem.

3. Mark a square on the top left corner of each of the top rectangles that begins 15 cm (6 in) from the top and 15 cm (6 in) from the side on the right side of the fabric. Repeat on the top right corner of both top rectangles.

4. With right sides facing up, align a top corner of one of your prepared sleeves with the square marked on the front top rectangle. Pin in place and repeat on the other side of the top rectangle. Repeat for both sleeves with the back top rectangle, and then try on the top and adjust the placement of the sleeves to suit you. Ideally, you'd like them to sit in a way that they don't slip off your shoulders. Make any adjustments to both sleeves so that everything is even. Once you are happy with the placement, topstitch the sleeves in place with a square.

5. Fold the top with the right sides together and sew up the side seams of the top and sleeves. Clip the seams under the arms (see page 51) to reduce bulk.

6. Hem the bottom of the top and ends of the sleeves (see page 73). Snip loose threads and press.

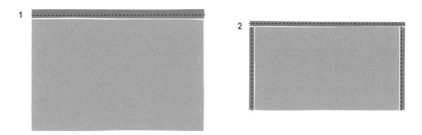

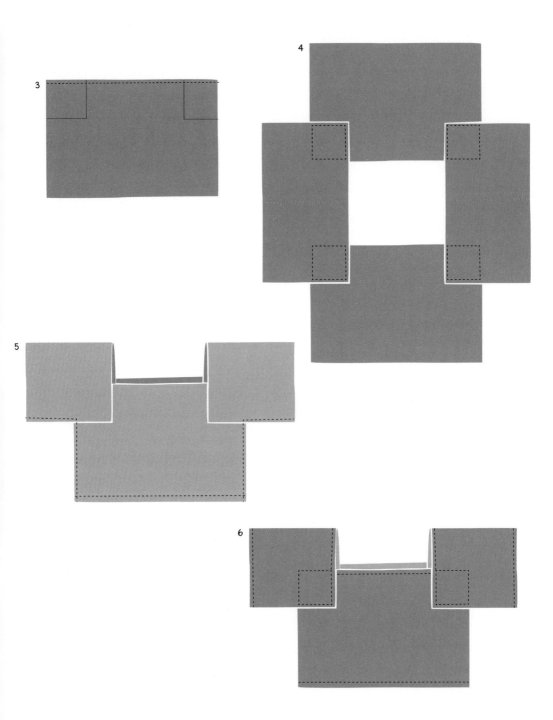

Variation

Balloon-Sleeve Dress

Transform a simple rectangular sleeve into a balloon sleeve with elastic! This hack can be applied to any of the projects with rectangle sleeves in this book.

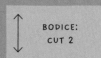

Bodice: cut 2

Width = Full bust ÷ 2 + 10 cm (4 in) + 2 cm (¾ in)

Height = High bust to belly button (includes seam allowance)

Sleeves: cut 2

Width = Top of shoulder to under bust x 2 + 2 cm (¾ in)

Height = Edge of shoulder to wrist + 2 cm (¾ in)

Skirt: cut 2

Width = Bodice width x 1.5 + 2 cm (¾ in)
Height = Belly button to desired length + 2 cm (¾ in)

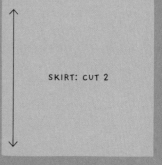

1–2 cm (½–¾ in) knit elastic for wristbands: cut 2

Length = Circumference of wrist + 2 cm (¾ in)

ELASTIC: CUT 2

1. Complete steps 1–5 of the Kama Square-Neck Top (see page 154) without hemming the bottom of the top. Sew and attach a long gathered skirt by following steps 6–7 of the Maya Ruffle Dress (see page 170).

2. Sew wristband casings and insert elastic at the end of each sleeve (see page 64).

3. Hem the bottom of the dress (see page 73). Snip loose threads and press.

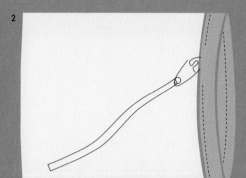

Pip Peplum Top

#diypippeplumtop

This project is based on the first DIY tutorial I ever shared: the Rectangle Dress. Usually, tops or dresses like this would use darts to shape the pattern piece to fit over the bust, but I love that this one uses gathers.

Straps: cut 2

5 cm (2 in) x 120 cm (47 ¼ in)

Top front: cut 2

Width = Full bust ÷ 2 + 3 cm (1 ¼ in) + 2 cm (¾ in)

Height = High bust to just below bust + 3 cm (1 ¼ in)

Top back: cut 2

Width = Same as top front

Height = Same as top front – 10 cm (4 in)

Peplum: cut 2

Width = Top width x 1.5 + 2 cm (¾ in)

Height = Under bust to hip (includes seam and hem allowance; the finished length will be below the waist but above the hip)

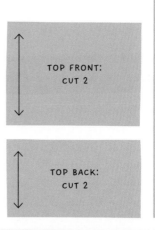

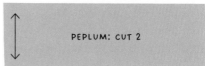

1. Fold each strap in half lengthways with the right sides together and pin. Sew a side seam along each strap, then turn out using a safety pin and iron flat. Cut a 12 cm (4 ¾ in) length from the end of each strap. These will become your strap loops.

2. Fold the strap loops in half and sew across the bottom to secure the ends.

3. With right sides together, place the loops 11 cm (4 ¼ in) in from each side on the top back, aligning the raw ends of the straps with the raw edge of the top rectangle, and pin them in place. Sew across the loops to secure them using a seam allowance of 5 mm (¼ in).

4. With right sides together, place the second top back on the first one, sandwiching the loops inside, and pin in place. This second rectangle will become the facing. Sew a straight stitch along the top edge.

5. Open up the fabric and spread it flat with right sides facing down and the strap loops underneath. Press the seam allowance up towards the facing and understitch it to the facing. Make sure you don't stitch through the strap loops. Fold the facing over so wrong sides are together and iron flat.

6. Repeat steps 3–5 with the top front pieces and the straps, though you will need to place the straps 12 cm (4 ¾ in) in from the sides. Pin and check their placement before stitching them down to make sure they are in a position you like.

7. Open out the top front and gather the side seams (see page 52). Open out the top back and adjust the gathers on the top front so the side seams are the same height as the side seams on the top back.

8. With right sides together, place the top back on the top front, pin and sew the side seams.

Continues overleaf.

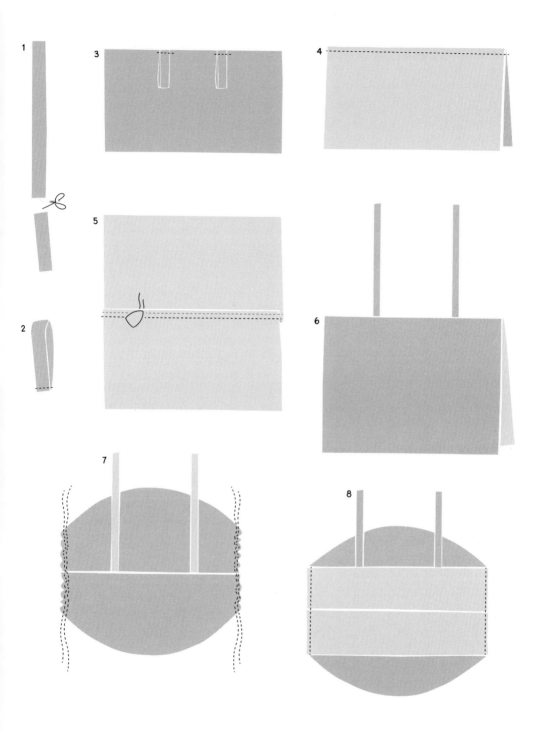

9. Fold the facing over to enclose all of the raw edges and press. Mark the centre front and back along the bottom edges of the top.

10. Place the peplum rectangles together with right sides facing and sew the side seams to create a loop. Mark the centre front and centre back of the peplum. Gather the top of the peplum loop (see page 52).

11. With right sides together, align the marks at centre front and centre back of the peplum loop with the marks on the top and pin. Align the side seams and pin. Spread the gathers evenly and tighten or loosen them as required until the circumference of the peplum is the same as the top. Pin and then sew a straight stitch to attach the peplum to the top.

12. Hem the bottom of the peplum (see page 73). Snip loose threads and press. To wear, thread the straps through the loops and tie them in a bow at the back.

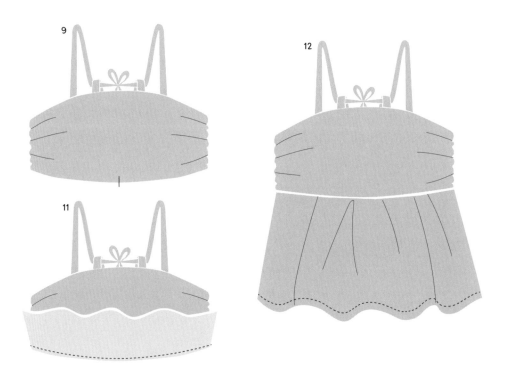

Variation

Tiered Gather Dress

What's better than one ruffle? TWO! Using the method below, you can add a second tier or even a third to any of your DIY creations. In the dress pictured page 167, I've added scrunchie straps (using the method on page 97).

PATTERN PIECES

Straps: cut 2

5 cm (2 in) x 120 cm (47 ¼ in)

Bodice front: cut 2

Use top front formula on page 161

Bodice back: cut 2

Use top back formula on page 161

Skirt first tier: cut 2

Width = Width of bodice front x 1.5 + 2 cm (¾ in)

Height = Waist to desired length ÷ 2 + 2 cm (¾ in)

Skirt second tier: cut 2

Width = Width of first tier x 1.5 + 2 cm (¾ in)
(if your fabric is not wide enough, join two rectangles together to get the required width)

Height = Top tier height + 2 cm (¾ in)

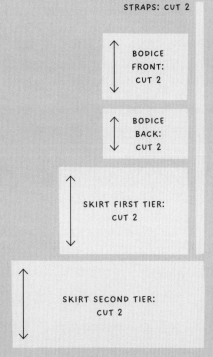

1. Complete steps 1–9 of the Pip Peplum Top (see pages 162–164).

2. Place the rectangles of the first tier right sides together and sew the side seams. Mark the centre front and centre back of the tier loop. Gather the top of the loop (see page 52). With right sides of the tier loop and bodice facing, align the marks at centre front and back of the loop to the marks on the bodice and pin. Align the side seams and pin. Spread the gathers evenly and tighten or loosen them as needed until the circumference of the tier loop is the same as the bodice. Pin and then sew a straight stitch to attach the first tier to the bodice.

3. Repeat step 2 with the second tier, gathering it to match the circumference of the first. Pin right sides together and then sew a straight stitch to attach the second tier to the first.

4. Hem the bottom of the skirt (see page 73). Snip loose threads and press. To wear, thread the straps through the loops and tie them in a bow at the back.

Maya Ruffle Dress

#diymayaruffledress

I designed this dress in Tokyo during a hot and humid summer, when I wanted something floaty and fun to wear. It can be altered in so many ways: you can lengthen the sleeves and add a casing to the wristband for a balloon sleeve moment, or transform it into an OTT crop top by leaving off the skirt.

Bodice: cut 2

Width = Arm bust (includes ease) ÷ 2 + 2 cm (¾ in)

Height = Top of shoulder to waist + 2 cm (¾ in)

Sleeves: cut 2

Width = Bodice rectangle height x 2 + 2 cm (¾ in) (or use the full width of the fabric)

Height = 25 cm (10 in) + 2 cm (¾ in)

Skirt: cut 2

Width = Bodice rectangle width x 2

Height = Waist to the desired length

Double fold bias binding for neckline: cut 1

Length = Up to 1 m (1 ⅛ yd) or enough to bind the neckline

Neckline template (see page 62)

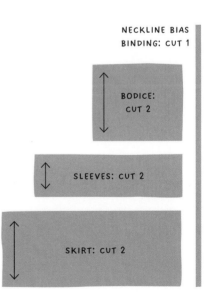

NECKLINE BIAS BINDING: CUT 1

BODICE: CUT 2

SLEEVES: CUT 2

SKIRT: CUT 2

1. Using the bodice rectangles and the bias binding, complete steps 1–4 of the Stephanie Rectangle-Sleeve Top (see page 132).

2. Mark the centre of both sleeve rectangles on the edge of the sleeve that you will attach to the bodice. Gather these edges on both rectangles (see page 52).

3. On the right side of the front and back of the bodice, mark 10 cm (4 in) up from the bottom on both edges.

4. With the right sides of the fabric together, align the centre mark on one of the gathered sleeve rectangles to a shoulder seam and pin. Match each end of the sleeve rectangle to the marks on the front and back of the bodice and pin. Spread the gathers evenly and tighten or loosen as required. Pin the remainder of the sleeve rectangle to the bodice and sew with a straight stitch. Repeat on the other side with the second sleeve.

5. Fold the bodice from the shoulder seams so that the right sides are facing and align the edges of the bodice and underarms of the sleeves. Pin and sew the side seams of the bodice and the underarm seams of the sleeves. Turn the bodice right side out and mark the centre front and back along the bottom edge.

6. Place the skirt rectangles together with right sides facing and sew the side seams to create a loop. Mark the centre front and centre back of the skirt loop. Gather the top edge of the skirt loop (see page 52).

7. With right sides together, align the centre marks on the skirt with the marks on the bodice and pin. Align the side seams and pin. Spread the gathers evenly and tighten or loosen as required until the circumference of the skirt loop is the same as the bodice. Pin and then sew a straight stitch to attach the skirt loop to the bodice.

8. Hem the sleeves and bottom of the dress (see page 73). Snip loose threads and press.

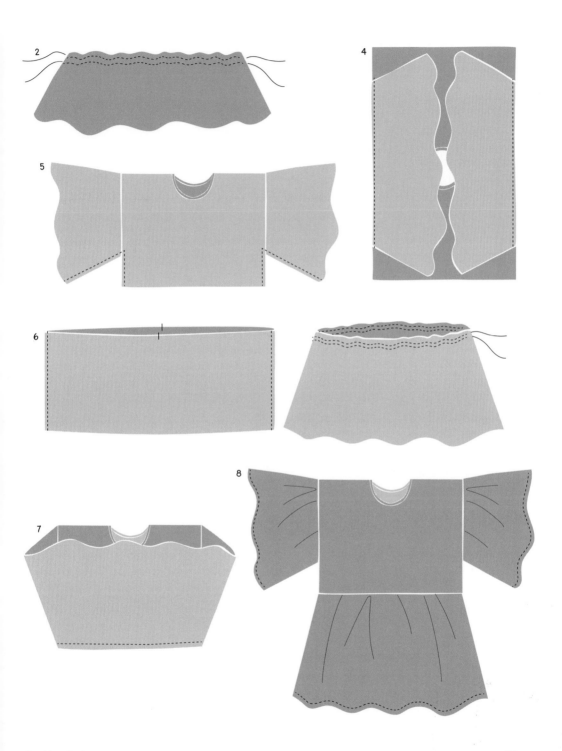

Variation

Wrap Bib

I love layering with interesting pieces to give dimension to an otherwise simple outfit. This Wrap Bib can be worn over a plain t-shirt, sweater or even a dress. As well as the fabric suggestions on pages 30–31, this works well in lightweight canvas, denim or twill, or even wool suiting.

PATTERN PIECES

TEMPLATE

Bib: cut 2

Width = Arm bust (includes seam allowance) − 10 cm (4 in) ÷ 2

Height = Top of shoulder to belly button + 2 cm (¾ in)

Sleeves: cut 2

Width = Bib rectangle height x 2 + 2 cm (¾ in)

Height = 30 cm (12 in) + 2 cm (¾ in)

Waist ties: cut 2

Width = 20 cm (8 in)

Length = Width of bib rectangle x 4

Double fold bias binding for neckline

Length = As long as neck opening

Double fold bias binding for sides of bib

Length = Height of bib x 4

Neckline template
(see page 62)

BIB:
CUT 2

SLEEVES: CUT 2

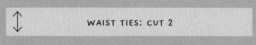

WAIST TIES: CUT 2

NECKLINE BIAS BINDING: CUT 1

SIDE BIB BIAS BINDING: CUT 1

1. Using the bib rectangles and bias binding for the neckline, complete steps 1–4 of the Stephanie Rectangle-Sleeve Top (see page 132).

2. On the right side of the fabric, mark the centre front and centre back of the bib along its bottom edge. Then on the front and back of the bib, mark 10 cm (4 in) up from the bottom on both sides.

3. Fold the sleeve rectangles in half with right sides facing and sew up the short ends. Trim the seam allowance, turn right side out and press. Mark the centre of each sleeve rectangle on the raw edge, which you will attach to the bib, and then gather that edge (see page 52), ensuring you sew through both layers. The ruffles will be double-sided, so you won't be able to see any hems when the bib is finished.

4. Sew each sleeve to the bib as described in step 4 of the Maya Ruffle Dress (see page 170). Press. Bind the raw edges on the sides of the bib with bias binding using the sandwich method (see page 59).

5. Turn the bib over so that the right side is facing down. Press the bias bound edge towards the bib and understitch the binding to the bib to stop it from rolling out.

6. Sew the waist ties by completing steps 1–4 of the Tie Belt (see page 100).

7. Mark the centre of each waist tie. Open up a waist tie and sandwich the bottom edge of the bib inside, matching the centre front of the bib to the centre of the tie. Pin and edgestitch along the top edge of the waist tie to attach it to the bib. Repeat with the second waist tie on the back of the bib. Snip loose threads and press.

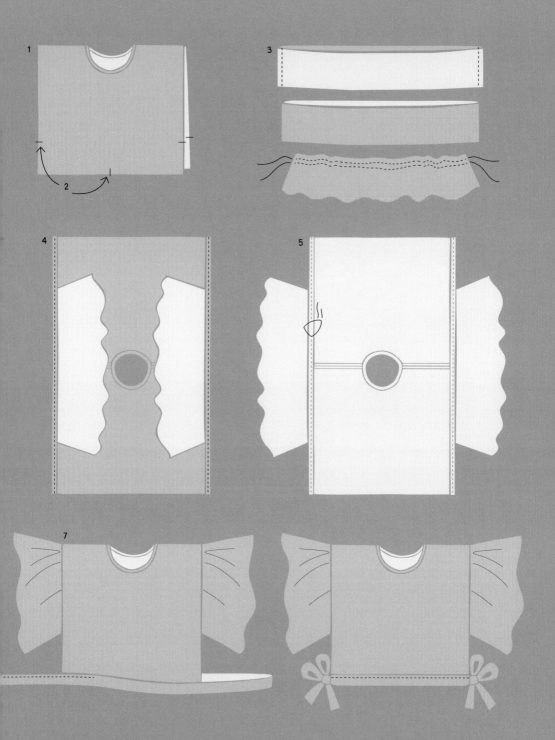

Sonya Ruffle Skirt

#diysonyaskirt

This skirt is one of my wardrobe staples and was the project I taught in my first ever sewing workshop. It has so many potential variations and looks great worn super casually with a t-shirt or dressed up. Shorten it to make a mini, add an asymmetric ruffle, or remove the ruffle altogether and add a split up the back.

Skirt: cut 2

Width = Hips ÷ 2 + 20 cm (8 in) + 2 cm (¾ in)

Height = Waist to knee (this includes the waistband casing and seam allowance; the finished length will be above the knee to allow you to walk properly)

Ruffle: cut 2

Width = Skirt rectangle width x 1.5 + 2 cm (¾ in)

Height = Knee to above ankle (includes seam and hem allowance)

2 ½ cm (1 in) non-roll elastic for waistband: cut 1

Length = Waist – 10–15 cm (4–6 in)

SKIRT: CUT 2

RUFFLE: CUT 2

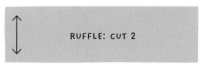

ELASTIC: CUT 1

1. Place front and back skirt rectangles together with right sides facing and sew the side seams to create a skirt loop. Mark the centre front and back along the bottom edge and turn the skirt loop right side out.

2. Place front and back skirt ruffles together with right sides facing and sew the side seams to create a ruffle loop. Mark the centre front and back on the top edge and turn the ruffle loop right side out. Gather the top edge (see page 52) so that the finished circumference is the same as the skirt loop.

3. With right sides facing, align the centre marks on the gathered ruffle loop with the marks on the skirt loop and pin. Align the side seams and pin. Spread the gathers evenly and tighten or loosen as required until the circumference of the ruffle loop is the same as the skirt loop. Pin and sew a straight stitch to attach the ruffle to the bottom of the skirt loop.

4. Sew a waistband casing and insert elastic on the top edge of the skirt (see page 64).

5. Hem the bottom of the skirt (see page 73). Snip loose threads and press.

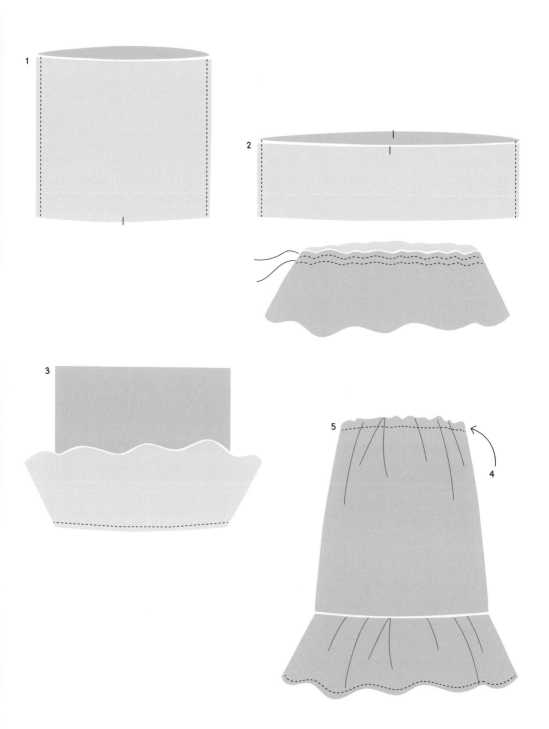

Double Ruffle Skirt

Add an extra ruffle for the ultimate salsa girl emoji moment!

PATTERN PIECES

Skirt: cut 2

Use skirt rectangles formula on page 177

Skirt ruffles: cut 4

Width = Skirt rectangle width x 1.5

Height = Knee to above ankle (includes seam
and hem allowance)

2 ½ cm (1 in) non-roll elastic for waistband: cut 1

Length = Waist – 10–15 cm (4–6 in)

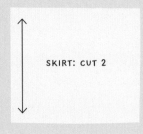

SKIRT: CUT 2

SKIRT RUFFLES: CUT 4

ELASTIC: CUT 1

1. Complete steps 1–5 of the Sonya Ruffle Skirt (see page 178). Cut the skirt loop in half widthways between 10 and 20 cm (4 and 8 in) above the ruffle. Mark the centre front and back on the upper part of the skirt loop.

2. Repeat step 2 of the Sonya Ruffle Skirt to create another ruffle loop and then step 3 to attach it to the upper half of the skirt loop.

3. Place the two pieces of the skirt loop right sides together, sandwiching the new ruffle between them. Align the side seams and pin, then sew a straight stitch to reattach the bottom section of the skirt. Snip loose threads and press.

Rosebud Raglan Top

#diyrosebudraglantop

This top was inspired by a 1960s vintage pattern I found at the op shop.
The original pattern was labelled 'one size fits all' but in modern sizing only
measured a size ten, so I drafted this version, using rectangles and my body
measurements, to come up with a formula that can be used to re-create it at
any size.

PATTERN PIECES

Top and sleeve rectangles: cut 4

Width = Arm bust (includes ease) ÷ 2 + 2 cm (¾ in)

Height = Top of shoulder to belly button + 2 cm (¾ in)

Armhole height (A) = Top of shoulder to full bust

1 cm (½ in) knit elastic for neckline: cut 1

Length = Measure the top edge of the neck hole
when the garment is lying flat + 10 cm (4 in)

1 cm (½ in) knit elastic for armbands: cut 2

Length = Measure around arm just above elbow

1 cm (½ in) knit elastic for bottom edge: cut 1

Length = Waist − 10–15 cm (4–6 in)

TOP AND SLEEVE
RECTANGLES: CUT 4

NECKLINE ELASTIC: CUT 1

ARMBAND ELASTIC: CUT 2

BOTTOM EDGE ELASTIC: CUT 1

1. Take one rectangle pattern piece and fold it in half widthways with right sides facing. First mark out the armhole. Measuring from the top corner, mark (A) down the side with the raw edges. Then measure 15 cm (6 in) along the top edge from the same corner and mark with chalk. Draw a curved line from the top mark to the bottom mark. I like to do this freehand, but you can use a bowl or tailor's curve if you prefer.

2. Cut along the line and then open out the fabric, laying it flat. Trace the armholes for the other three pattern pieces from this piece and cut. Mark two pattern pieces with chalk to indicate that they are the sleeves.

3. With right sides facing, place a sleeve on one of the top pattern pieces, align the edges of the armholes and pin. Sew the sleeve to the top with a straight stitch. Repeat with the other sleeve on the opposite side of the top piece.

4. Fold the sleeves in half with wrong sides facing and then place the remaining pattern piece on top so the right sides of top and sleeve are facing and the armholes match up. Pin the sleeves to the second top piece and then sew with a straight stitch.

5. Fold the top right sides together, align the side seams of top and sleeves and pin. Sew the side seams of the top and the underarms of the sleeves with a straight stitch.

6. Turn the top right side out. Sew casings on the neckline, sleeve ends and bottom edge of the top and insert elastic (see page 64). Snip loose threads and press.

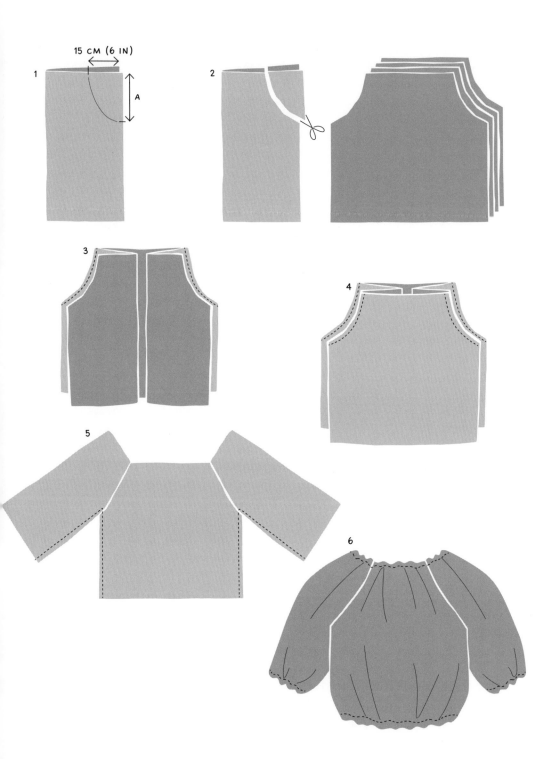

Variation

Raglan Dress

Sleeves not big enough? Here's how to transform your Rosebud Raglan Top into a super puffy sleeved extravaganza. In this variation the formula will give you a mini dress that you can pair, if you like, with a Tie Belt (see page 99).

PATTERN PIECES

Dress: cut 2

Width = Body measurement at widest point (hips, bust or tummy) ÷ 2 + 20 cm (8 in)

Height = Top of shoulder to desired length + 2 cm (¾ in)

Armhole height (A) = Top of shoulder to full bust

Sleeves: cut 2

Width = Width of dress rectangle x 1.5 + 2 cm (¾ in)

Height = Top of shoulder to desired length + 10 cm (4 in) + 2 cm (¾ in)

Armhole height (A) = Top of shoulder to full bust

1 cm (½ in) knit elastic for neckline: cut 1

Length = Measure the top edge of the neck hole when the garment is lying flat + 10 cm (4 in)

1 cm (½ in) knit elastic for armbands: cut 2

Length = Measure around arm where you would like the sleeve to end

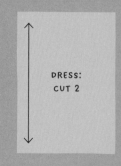

DRESS: CUT 2

SLEEVES: CUT 2

NECKLINE ELASTIC: CUT 1

ARMBAND ELASTIC: CUT 2

1. Take one of the dress rectangles and fold it in half widthways with right sides facing. First mark out the armhole. Measuring from the top corner, mark (A) down the side with the raw edges. Then measure 15 cm (6 in) along the top edge from the same corner and mark with chalk. Draw a curved line from the top mark to the bottom mark. I like to do this freehand, but you can use a bowl or tailor's curve if you prefer.

2. Cut along the line and then open out the fabric, laying it flat. Trace and cut the armholes for the second dress rectangle and the sleeve rectangles from this piece.

3. Complete steps 3–5 of the Rosebud Raglan Top (see page 186).

4. Sew casings on the neckline and sleeve ends and insert elastic (see page 64). Hem the bottom of the dress (see page 73). Snip loose threads and press.

15см

1

A

2

4

Trace Dress

#diytracedress

There's a dress I sewed using the trace method that has to be one of my most-worn me-made creations. I made it to take with me on a holiday and ended up wearing it almost every day. It's such a simple shape but a go-to when I'm not sure what to wear. You can make a Trace Dress from any loose-fitting t-shirt. Hack the Trace Dress by turning it into a peplum top.

A loose-fitting t-shirt

Enough fabric to trace around the t-shirt twice and add ease and seam allowance

Enough fabric for a gathered skirt (see Maya Ruffle Dress, page 169)

Double fold bias binding for neckline as long as neck opening

Neckline template (see page 62)

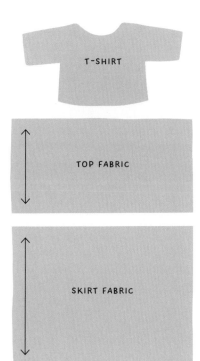

NECKLINE BIAS BINDING

1. Fold the fabric in half with the right sides together. Fold the t-shirt in half and lay it on the fabric, aligning the fold of the t-shirt with the fold on the fabric. Trace around the t-shirt, take the t-shirt away and then draw a second line around the shoulder and down the side seam 5 cm (2 in) outside the first for ease and seam allowance. Curve the line under the arm. Trace the neckline or use your neckline template to mark out the neck hole. Cut out the front piece and then unfold it and lay it on the fabric to cut out the back piece.

2. Place the front and back pieces together with right sides facing. Pin and then sew one shoulder seam.

3. Bind the neckline with bias binding using the sandwich method or facing method (see page 59 or 60).

4. Put the front and back pieces together again with right sides facing. Pin and then sew the other shoulder seam.

5. Fold the bodice from the shoulder seams, right sides together. Pin and sew the side seams on the bodice and under the arms.

6. Attach a gathered skirt to the bodice by completing steps 6–7 of the Maya Ruffle Dress (see page 170).

7. Hem the sleeves and bottom of the dress (see page 73). Snip loose threads and press.

Variation

Keyhole Top

Apply this keyhole cut-out hack to any top or dress in the book. Trace the keyhole templates on the inside cover or draft your own. The Keyhole Top is pictured on page 58.

YOU WILL NEED

A loose-fitting t-shirt

Enough fabric to trace around the t-shirt twice and add ease and seam allowance

Double fold bias binding for keyhole as long as keyhole opening

Double fold bias binding for neckline 3–4 times as long as neck hole

TEMPLATE

Keyhole template (see inside cover)

1. After completing step 1 of the Trace Dress (see page 194), fold the back pattern piece in half with right sides together. Align your chosen keyhole template with the centre fold, trace the template and then cut out the keyhole.

2. Bind the keyhole with bias binding using the sandwich method (see page 59).

3. Place the front and back pieces of the top with right sides together. Pin and sew the shoulder seams.

4. Mark the centre of the neck hole binding and the centre front of the top.

5. Match the centre marks and pin the binding to the neckline, sandwiching the raw edge between the bias binding. Stitch the binding to the neckline, starting at one end of the binding and sewing around the neckline all the way to the other end. Tie each end of the binding into a tiny knot.

6. Complete the top by following step 5 of the Trace Dress and hemming the bottom and sleeves of the top.

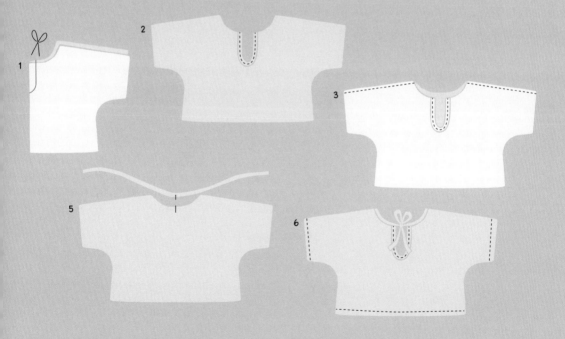

Trace Pants

#diytracepants

Tracing clothing you already have is a great way to DIY your wardrobe, the logic being that if the original piece fits you then so should your traced creation. I love a high-waisted fit; for this project, you will need a pair of loose-fitting, high-waisted pants made from woven fabric to trace. This version has an elastic waistband and lots of added ease, so the final result is an oversized, comfy pair of pants. Use this method to make culottes or shorts too! These best suit lightweight and midweight linen or canvas and midweight cotton.

PANTS

YOU WILL NEED

A pair of loose-fitting, high-waisted pants

Enough fabric to trace around the pants twice and add ease and seam allowance

2 ½ cm (1 in) elastic = Waist − 10 cm (4 in)

FABRIC

ELASTIC

1. First trace the back of the pants. Fold the fabric in half with the right sides together. Fold the pants in half with the front sides facing and lay them on the fabric. Trace around the pants with chalk, take the pants away and then draw a second line 5 cm (2 in) outside the first for ease and seam allowance. You will also need to allow for a casing for the elastic waistband, calculated using this casing formula: width of elastic x 2 + 1 cm (½ in). Add that measurement to the top of the pants.

2. To trace the front piece, fold the pants in half with the back sides facing and lay them on the fabric. Trace around the pants, and then draw a second line 5 cm (2 in) outside the first for ease and seam allowance, plus the allowance for the waistband casing.

3. Before cutting out the pattern pieces, check that the length of the inseam (the inside leg) and the side seam of the pants are the same length on both pieces and adjust if necessary until they match. Mark (B) for back and (F) for front on the pattern pieces to identify them, then cut out the pattern pieces.

4. Place one of the back and one of the front pieces together with right sides facing and sew the side seam. Repeat with the other front and back pieces so that you have two separate leg pieces.

5. Place the back pieces together with right sides facing and sew the centre back seam. Place the front pieces together with right sides facing and sew the centre front seam.

6. Match up the centre front and back inseams at the crotch and sew the inseam on each leg.

7. Create a waistband casing and insert elastic along the top edge (see page 64).

8. Hem the bottom of the pant legs (see page 73). Snip loose threads and press.

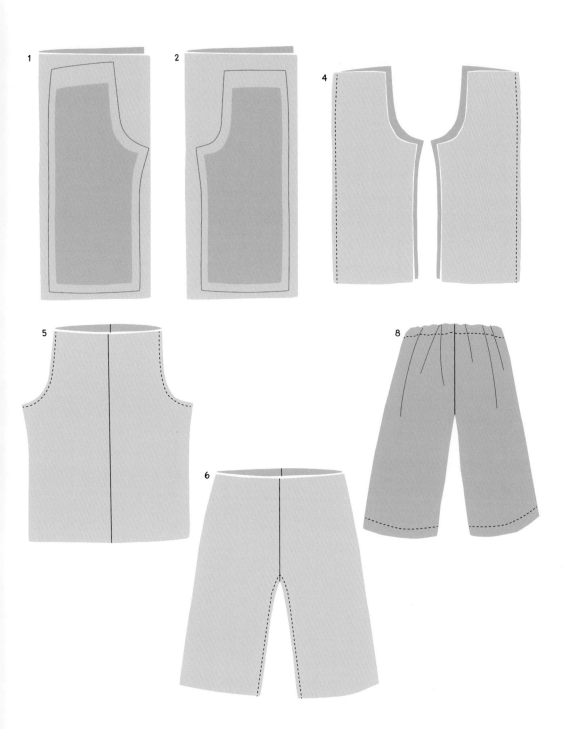

Patch Pocket Shorts

You can't have a pair of shorts without a patch pocket on the back! Add one in a contrasting fabric for a cheeky detail or practise your print-matching skills and stitch a hidden one.

YOU WILL NEED

A pair of loose-fitting, high-waisted shorts

Enough fabric to trace around the shorts twice and add ease and seam allowance

Fabric to create a patch pocket (see page 70)

2 ½ cm (1 in) elastic = Waist – 10 cm (4 in)

1. Complete steps 1–8 of the Trace Pants (see page 200) using a pair of shorts as a template.

2. Try on the shorts and place your hand on your bum where you'd like to put the pocket. Mark with chalk and then remove the shorts.

3. Create a patch pocket by completing steps 1–6 on page 71. Pin the pocket onto the shorts using your chalk markings as a guide while making sure the edge of the pocket is parallel with the side seam. Check the pocket's placement by trying on the shorts with the pins holding it in place. Just be careful not to prick yourself!

4. Once you are happy with the placement, stitch it in place as per step 7 of the patch pocket tutorial on page 71.

Resources

Fabrics

The outfits featured in the photographs throughout this book were made with fabrics generously supplied by the following fabric stores.

The Fabric Store (New Zealand, Australia and online) thefabricstoreonline.com

Established in 1995, The Fabric Store is a destination point for the sewing and creative community, offering a curated range of designer dress fabrics and mill overruns.

Blackbird Fabrics (online) blackbirdfabrics.com

Curated for sewists by sewists, Blackbird Fabrics is a Canadian online fabric store offering a range of modern, high-quality garment fabrics.

The Strawberry Thief (Australia and online) thestrawberrythief.com.au

Distributing from Fremantle, Western Australia, The Strawberry Thief is the Southern Hemisphere's largest online retailer and wholesaler of Liberty Tana Lawn to the quilt and craft industry.

Tessuti Fabrics (Australia and online) tessuti-shop.com

Located in Sydney and Melbourne and available online, Tessuti Fabrics has been selling beautiful designer fabrics since 1992.

The Fine Cloth Company (New Zealand and online) thefineclothcompany.co.nz

With a mission to inspire individuality and style through fabric, The Fine Cloth Company offers a colourful range of wools, linens and silks.

A & R Fabrics (Australia and online)
aandrfabrics.com

With a strong focus on natural fibres, A & R Fabrics stocks a small but seriously beautiful collection of dress fabrics, perfect for home sewists.

Woven labels

Kylie & the Machine (online)
kylieandthemachine.shop

High-quality woven labels to complete your handmade items – the signature to finish your artwork!

Further reading

Modern Mending: Minimise waste and maximise style by Erin Lewis Fitzgerald

Learn how to bring new life to or extend the life of your handmade clothes with this fun and easy guide to modern mending.

The Act of Sewing: How to make and modify clothes to wear every day by Sonya Philip

The book I wish I had when I started sewing. This in-depth guide includes four simple patterns and encourages you to make a wardrobe all your own.

Make It Simple: Easy, speedy sewing projects to stitch up in an afternoon by Tilly Walnes

Sewing shouldn't be stressful and this book makes it easy, with six beginner projects to build your me-made wardrobe.

Listening

Love to Sew Podcast
lovetosewpodcast.com

This podcast is one of my favourite things to listen to while I create, helping me feel inspired and connected to other makers who share my love of sewing.

Thank You

I never dreamed that my DIY journey would include writing a book, and it would not have been possible without the support of many crafty and creative people. THANK YOU!

Thank you to my little sister, Amaya, for being patient with me, recognising when I needed a bubble tea break and being the best photoshoot helper ever. My twin sister, Aurora, for always answering my calls, reminding me to stay positive, and encouraging all my crazy outfit ideas. My parents, David and Kiri, for making sure I was fed and for getting excited about every single update. My little brother, David, for painting the props and making sure the beer fridge stayed stocked up. To our cat, Raisen, for personally ensuring every garment in this book was covered in cat hair.

Chloe Chalk, for reading the first draft of my manuscript, being my unofficial editor, taking me on walks and getting me out of the studio. Samantha Ashe, Rebecca Petersen and Miranda Parsons for being the ultimate hype girls and reminding me to be myself.

Megan Boxsell, Mel Tesch and Jac Duong, the most amazing sewing cheer squad, for being there for all the highs and lows from day one of writing, all the way up until the photoshoot and beyond. Thank you for snipping threads, ironing creases and capturing all the BTS fun. You are a dream team!

Elle Ninness, Giverny Hay, Kylie Lakay, Jessica Cook and Maddie Bell for being way more than just models. Thank you for bringing all of your fabulous energy to help make the photo shoot a success and for making my DIY creations come to life.

Kitiya Palaskas, Rachel Burke and Sha'an d'Anthes for sharing your book-making experience with me – I would have been lost without your insight and inspiration!

Elizabeth Baumgart for recommending an incredible photographer. Rod Pillbeam for capturing all of the DIY madness that was inside my brain and making everything look wondrous.

To the fabric companies who generously provided the fabrics featured in the book: Tracy and Grace at The Fine Cloth Company, Colette at Tessuti Fabrics, Jasmine and the team at The Fabric Store, Trin at A & R Fabrics, Caroline at Blackbird Fabrics and Robyn at The Strawberry Thief. Thank you for your generosity on this project.

Kristen Devitt of Each to Own and Tiffany Atkin of Shibuya Moon for providing the fabbest earrings to style with all of our outfits.

Emily Hart for being the smiliest face on the other side of a webcam. From day one you have been so patient and open to my ideas. From aprons to earrings, you got all my references and have made my DIY dreams come true. Eugenie Baulch, for your attention to detail and for absolutely transforming these pages into a real book. Sinéad Murphy for taking a mood board and making magic! Thank you for creating the things I see in my mind and putting them on paper.

Ngaire Harman, my high school art teacher, for always being so supportive of my ideas and creative expression. I wouldn't be making or sharing my craft today if it wasn't for you letting me bring a sewing machine into the art room at school.

To the sewing community, thank YOU for flipping open the pages and giving this book a read. I hope it inspires you to DIY the things you dream about.

Published in 2022 by Hardie Grant Books, an imprint of Hardie Grant Publishing

Hardie Grant Books (Melbourne)
Wurundjeri Country
Building 1, 658 Church Street
Richmond, Victoria 3121

Hardie Grant Books (London)
5th & 6th Floors
52–54 Southwark Street
London SE1 1UN

hardiegrant.com/au/books

 A catalogue record for this book is available from the National Library of Australia

NATIONAL LIBRARY OF AUSTRALIA

Sew It Yourself
ISBN 978 1 74379 820 1

10 9 8 7 6

Commissioning Editor: Emily Hart
Editor: Eugenie Baulch
Design Manager: Kristin Thomas
Designer and Illustrator: Sinéad Murphy, Lovelock
Make-up: Shannon Jennings
Production Manager: Todd Rechner
Production Coordinator: Jessica Harvie

Colour reproduction by Splitting Image Colour Studio
Printed in China by Leo Paper Products LTD.

Hardie Grant acknowledges the Traditional Owners of the country on which we work, the Wurundjeri people of the Kulin nation and the Gadigal people of the Eora nation, and recognises their continuing connection to the land, waters and culture. We pay our respects to their Elders past and present.